STERLING BIOGRAPHIES

ABRAHAM LINCOLN

From Pioneer to President

E.B. Phillips

STERLING

New York / London
www.sterlingpublishing.com/kids

For my father
Robert Ferguson Phillips
with love

STERLING and the distinctive Sterling logo are registered trademarks of
Sterling Publishing Co., Inc.

Library of Congress Cataloging-in-Publication Data
Phillips, E. B. (Ellen Blue)
   Abraham Lincoln : from pioneer to president / E.B. Phillips.
      p. cm.   (Sterling biographies)
   Includes bibliographical references and index.
   ISBN 978-1-4027-3396-3
   1. Lincoln, Abraham, 1809-1865--Juvenile literature. 2. Presidents--United States--
Biography--Juvenile literature. I. Title.

E457.905.P48 2007
973.7092--dc22
[B]

                                                                          2006027148

10 9 8 7 6 5 4

Published by Sterling Publishing Co., Inc.
387 Park Avenue South, New York, NY 10016
© 2007 by E.B. Phillips
Distributed in Canada by Sterling Publishing
c/o Canadian Manda Group, 165 Dufferin Street
Toronto, Ontario, Canada M6K 3H6
Distributed in the United Kingdom by GMC Distribution Services
Castle Place, 166 High Street, Lewes, East Sussex, England BN7 1XU
Distributed in Australia by Capricorn Link (Australia) Pty. Ltd.
P.O. Box 704, Windsor, NSW 2756, Australia

Printed in China
All rights reserved

Sterling ISBN 978-1-4027-3396-3 (paperback)

Sterling ISBN 978-1-4027-4745-8 (hardcover)

Designed by Joe Borzetta
Image research by Susan Schader

For information about custom editions, special sales, premium and
corporate purchases, please contact Sterling Special Sales
Department at 800-805-5489 or specialsales@sterlingpublishing.com.

Contents

Events in the Life of Abraham Lincoln

February 12, 1809
Abraham Lincoln is born near Elizabethtown, Kentucky.

1831
At the age of 22, Abraham leaves his family to explore life on his own. He moves to New Salem, Illinois.

1832
Abraham decides to run for Illinois State Legislature and loses, but is elected as officer of his militia in the Black Hawk War.

1833
Abolitionists organize the American Antislavery Society, led by William Lloyd Garrison.

1834
Lincoln again runs for Illinois State Legislature and this time easily wins the election.

1836
Lincoln is reelected into the State Legislature and moves to Springfield, the new capital of Illinois.

November 4, 1842
Lincoln marries Mary Ann Todd of Lexington.

1846
Lincoln is elected to the U.S. Congress and moves to Washington in November of 1847.

January 1849
Lincoln announces he will introduce a congressional bill to abolish slavery.

October 4, 1854
Lincoln makes his first great speech at the Springfield State Fair. There he publicly establishes his antislavery platform.

March 6, 1857
The Dred Scott Decision, which declared that Congress could not outlaw slavery in the territories, brings America closer to civil war.

1860
Lincoln gives a moving speech at Cooper Institute in New York City, which casts him in a favorable light. He is nominated for presidential candidate at the National Republican Convention in Chicago and wins the election on November 7.

December 20, 1860
South Carolina leads the southern states' secession, and the Confederate States of America are formed.

March 4, 1861
Lincoln is inaugurated as the 16th president of the United States.

April 12, 1861
The Civil War begins when the southern states attack Fort Sumter.

January 1, 1863
Abraham Lincoln signs the Emancipation Proclamation, which stated that all slaves in rebellious states were free. Many former slaves join the Union army.

November 1864
Lincoln is elected for a second term as president.

December 6, 1865
Urged by Lincoln, Congress passes the 13th Amendment to the Constitution, guaranteeing freedom for all slaves forever.

April 3, 1865
Richmond, the capital of the Confederacy, falls to the Union armies. The Civil War ends.

April 14, 1865
Lincoln is shot by John Wilkes Booth at a theater performance. He dies on the morning of April 15.

1809

1865

The Self-Taught President

I happen temporarily to occupy this big White House. I am living witness that any one of your children may look to come here as my father's child has.

F ew American presidents are as revered as Abraham Lincoln. He guided the nation through its terrible civil war. He freed four million African Americans from slavery with the Emancipation Proclamation—and paid for his beliefs with his life. It's no wonder that the details of Lincoln's life are often overshadowed by the legends of his greatness.

The details of Lincoln's life are fascinating. Reared in poverty on the Illinois frontier, Lincoln worked from the age of eight—as a laborer, soldier, postman, and shopkeeper. While he worked, he educated himself. He taught himself grammar and became a talented orator. He taught himself geometry and became a skilled surveyor. He taught himself law and became a successful young attorney.

This discipline helped Lincoln face the challenges of his presidency. When he was elected in 1860, he had held only one national office, so he had to learn his job quickly while his country—North versus South—exploded into war. Lincoln had political enemies, even in his own army. His family life was stormy and tragic.

But Lincoln met each of these challenges. He became a wise leader—perhaps America's greatest president.

CHAPTER 1

A Boy in the Backwoods

[He] had an axe put into his hands at once. From that till within his twenty-third year, he was almost constantly handling that most useful instrument.

Early in the winter of 1816, a two-horse wooden wagon piled with featherbeds rolled north along the bumpy Wilderness Road that led from Kentucky through Indiana and on to Illinois. In the wagon rode Thomas Lincoln, a farmer and carpenter; his wife, Nancy Hanks; his nine-year-old daughter, Sarah; and "a tall spider of a boy"—his seven-year-old son, Abraham, who had been born on February 12, 1809, near Elizabethtown, Kentucky.

The family had become pioneers because Thomas Lincoln's right to his Kentucky farmland was in dispute. In addition, Kentucky was a slave state, and the Lincolns believed that slavery was wrong. But in the wild woods of the Indiana Territory, slavery was illegal, and the U.S. government was selling carefully surveyed land with undisputed rights for two dollars an acre. The opportunity looked good to Thomas Lincoln, and he staked a claim to 160 acres of Indiana forest. In December 1816—the same time Indiana became a state—he loaded his wife and children into the wagon and set off for Little Pigeon Creek, Indiana, a small town about seventeen miles north of the Ohio River.

The 100-mile trip took two weeks. The family put up a three-sided lean-to as a shelter from the winter winds and the wolves that howled at night.

Sleeping in the shelter, living on the meat of the wild turkeys and deer that Thomas shot, the family got to work. Abraham, as he would later write of himself, "had an axe put into his hands at once. From that till within his twenty-third year, he was almost constantly handling that most useful instrument." Through the short winter days, Abraham helped his father cut trees, clear underbrush, and build a cabin, which was finished a few days after Abraham's eighth birthday. The cabin had

I believe that Government by the People, and for the People, will not perish from the Earth.

A. Lincoln

This 1892 calendar displays Lincoln's portrait and an illustration of the log cabin where he was born near Elizabethtown, Kentucky.

one room—twenty feet long and eighteen feet wide—a stone fireplace, and a dirt floor. Pegs in the wall served as a ladder to the loft where Abraham slept.

Over the next few years, the family toiled away at their farm. The boy and his father cleared the land; put in corn, wheat, oats, cotton, and flax; and traded their crops for farm animals—hogs, chickens, cows, and sheep. They grew or raised all of their own food. Nancy and Sarah made all their clothes from buckskins tanned on the farm and from homespun fabric created from the cotton and flax that they picked, carded, spun, and wove.

The Lincolns weren't alone for long. Other pioneers came to the region, and within a year, Nancy's aunt and uncle and her nineteen-year-old cousin Dennis settled nearby. A jovial boy, Dennis became Abraham's friend. Whenever there was time off from farm labor, they explored the woods and competed in running, jumping, and wrestling.

Then, in the summer of 1818, disaster struck. The family cows grazed on a toxic weed called white snakeroot, poisoning their milk. People who drank the milk sank into a coma and died. Nancy nursed her aunt and uncle when they fell ill, but she too came down with "milk sickness," and within a week, she was dead.

The children were stunned. Abraham never talked much about it, but years later he would write, "In this sad world of ours,

A photograph, c. 1891, shows the fireplace in the original cabin where Lincoln grew up. Mrs. Lincoln's spinning wheel sits next to the hearth.

sorrow comes to all; and to the young it comes with bitterest agony, because it takes them unawares. I have had experience enough to know what I say."

A New Mother

Without affectionate, hard-working Nancy, the family fell into a depression. All the traditional "women's work"—from weaving to washing—fell to Sarah. But Sarah was only twelve, and she found it difficult to keep up.

Thomas Lincoln left the children with Dennis and rode back to Kentucky, where he

In this 19th-century wood engraving, a sad young Abraham is depicted visiting his mother's grave after her untimely death in 1818.

found a new wife in an old friend—the widowed mother of two girls and a boy. Her name was Sarah Bush Johnston, but most people called her Sally.

When Sally and her children arrived at Little Pigeon Creek, they found a sad-looking, dirty cabin and two sad, grimy, hungry children dressed in rags. An energetic, sweet-natured person, Sally got right to work. She made Thomas build a wooden floor for the cabin and put in a window; she cleaned and cooked, and sewed new clothes for Sarah and Abraham.

Sally brought energy and love into the little house, which was now home to eight people. Although she could not read or write, she opened new vistas for Abraham. She had three books—*Dilworth's Spelling Book*, *Robinson Crusoe*, and *The Arabian Nights*—that she shared with him.

Sally had a special feeling for Abraham. She saw the intelligent child's thirst for learning. He'd had no more than a year's teaching at the informal schools that had sprung up in Kentucky and Indiana settlements, but he was determined to educate himself. He "read all the books he could lay his hands on," Sally would later recall, "and when he came across a passage that Struck him he would write it down on boards if he had no paper & keep it there until he did get paper—then he would rewrite it." Abraham borrowed books from neighbors, and would read the Bible, biographies of George Washington and Ben Franklin, as well as spelling, arithmetic, and elocution textbooks.

This intense study was one of the things that set Abraham apart from the other people of Little

Thomas Lincoln was a hard-working man who never approved of or understood his son Abraham's desire for education and knowledge.

This undated wood engraving of Sarah Bush Lincoln shows Abraham's stepmother at the age of 76. She was the first to nurture his love of reading.

Pigeon Creek, where few could read well. The busy settlers had little time for reading. They farmed their homesteads from sunrise to sundown, and when they saw the boy with a book in his hand, they called him "lazy." "He was always reading, scribbling, writing, ciphering, writing poetry," a relative remarked.

He "read all the books he could lay his hands on."

Abraham's father, Thomas Lincoln, was a hard-working, hospitable man, and a good neighbor. He was renowned for his hunting skill. He was famous, too, for his physical strength and for his storytelling—skills that Abraham shared. However, Thomas could barely sign his name, and he was not pleased with Abraham. He disapproved of Abraham's bookishness and dislike of farm work. Abraham's cousin Dennis Hanks said that Abraham was "a Constant, and I m[a]y Say Stubborn reader, his father having sometimes to slash him for neglecting his work by reading." A neighbor said that Thomas Lincoln "never showed by his actions that he thought much of his son Abraham when a boy."

The feeling seemed to be mutual. Abraham never had a kind word to say about Thomas Lincoln, and years later, when the old man was dying, Abraham refused to visit him.

This 19th-century American lithograph depicts young Abraham with his nose in a book while carrying his axe to work.

Following His Own Path

Despite his preference for reading, as a boy Abraham did the farm work that was demanded of him. Thomas often hired him out to neighbors or to work the ferries on the Ohio, taking his wages for his family.

Abraham's love of reading wasn't the only thing that set him apart from the others. Unlike the men he knew, he didn't hunt. Once when he was eight, he shot a wild turkey through a chink in the cabin walls, and the bird's death chilled him: "[I have] never since pulled a trigger on any larger game," he wrote.

Even as a teenager, he went his own way. Most men smoked or chewed tobacco in those days, but he didn't. Most men drank. Abraham didn't, but he wouldn't condemn drinkers or join one of the many temperance (anti-alcohol) societies. Most people joined a church. Abraham never did. He was wary of organized religion.

Most people joined a church. Abraham never did. He was wary of organized religion.

Still, he was well liked. He was tall and strong— a good runner, jumper, and wrestler. He was friendly company, with a wonderful sense of humor and a huge collection of stories and jokes. "He was the most entertaining person I ever knew," said a friend.

A New World to See

The Little Pigeon Creek years passed in a seasonal round of sowing and reaping, happiness and sorrow. Abraham's sister, Sarah, who was almost a mother to him, got married. But in January 1828, when Abraham was almost nineteen, she died during childbirth.

In April, his grief was eased when an opportunity arose that

Young Abraham steers his flatboat down the river to New Orleans in this 20th-century painting by Louis Bonhajo.

would allow him to see the world. A storekeeper named James Gentry hired him to help his son, Allen, take a flatboat loaded with farm produce down to New Orleans.

They poled south with the current. The route took them down the Ohio River, then down the vast Mississippi River, until they reached the southern woods of New Orleans. Abraham was amazed at what he saw. More than a thousand flatboats, heavy with western farm goods, lined the docks. Slaves loaded their produce onto sailing ships that would take it all over the world. After the boys sold their load, they saw the sights—the elegant houses of the **French Quarter,** the carriages, the women in their silks. They even observed the grim slave markets where people were sold like animals.

Slave Auctions

During Lincoln's lifetime, slave auctions in the South were commonplace. They provided a marketplace where plantation owners could purchase black slaves to work in their fields. Posters around town advertised the upcoming auction.

Upon arriving on a slave ship, Africans taken against their will were herded into a small cell and cleaned up. The males were greased to give their skin a healthy appearance. And to show their status as a slave, each was branded with a hot iron.

The slaves were then brought to a platform for inspection and the bidding would begin. Slave owners looked for the healthiest specimens and would prod and inspect the slaves, trying to determine which were the best ones. Women slaves were also placed in the auction, and often families were split apart as they were sold to different owners.

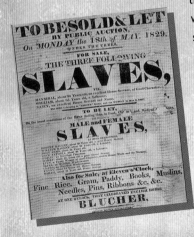

A large 1829 poster announces an upcoming slave auction where both male and female slaves are to be sold.

Allen and Abraham returned to Pigeon Creek by steamboat. For his three months of work, Abraham earned twenty-five dollars, which he turned over to his father.

In March of 1830, the Lincoln clan—now thirteen strong, thanks to the marriages of Sally's daughters—moved West. They had done well in Indiana, but Illinois was fresh territory with rich prairie soil. Thomas sold his farm, and off they went in three covered wagons.

They settled in central Illinois, near the Sangamon River. Abraham once again helped his father build a house and break the prairie sod to get to the rich black soil.

Allen and Abraham returned to Pigeon Creek by steamboat. For his three months of work, Abraham earned twenty-five dollars, which he turned over to his father.

The first winter was terrible. Survivors called it the winter of the "Deep Snow." In late December, a blizzard blanketed the prairie with three feet of snow. During the next two months, the temperature stayed at twelve below zero, and people ran short of food as their livestock starved. While trapped in the cabin, Abraham made plans to strike out on his own. When spring came, he would head for New Orleans again. A wider world was calling.

CHAPTER 2

On His Own in New Salem

If any man thinks I am a coward, let him test it.

When Abraham Lincoln left his family to explore life on his own at the age of twenty-two, he was, in his own words, "a strange, friendless, uneducated, penniless boy, working on a flatboat at ten dollars per month."

At first, people in the little settlement of New Salem, Illinois, did find him strange. Young Abraham was a bony, awkward, homely fellow, six feet four inches tall—much taller than most men then—with very long arms, very large feet, and a head of unruly black hair. He wore a thin jacket too short to cover his middle and jeans that left six inches of his long legs bare. He was, one man said, "as ruff a specimen of humanity as could be found."

These were strong words coming from a rough frontier town like New Salem. With a population of about a hundred people, it served as a meeting place for farmers within a

Lacking social graces but a model of strength and hard work, Abraham Lincoln could split rails with ease as shown in this oil painting, c. 1858.

fifteen-mile radius. New Salem had a post office, two doctors, a tavern where people could lodge, two saloons, and a couple of general stores that sold the few items that people couldn't make for themselves. It also had a mill that ground the farmers' wheat and corn.

Proving Himself in New Salem

It was the mill that gave people their first look at Abraham Lincoln. The mill pond had been made by damming the Sangamon River just below the town. Abraham, along with his stepbrother, his cousin, and a merchant named Denton Offutt, approached the dam one afternoon in May of 1831. They were poling a flatboat loaded with corn, barrels of pork, and pens of squealing hogs and they were heading for the Illinois and Mississippi rivers, which would take them to New Orleans. When they tried to run over the dam the boat got stuck on top, stern down in the river, so that water poured in.

It looked like a disaster, and everyone in town came out to watch. They saw lanky young Abraham take over. He got the men to shift some goods to shore and some to the bow of the boat to balance it. He borrowed a drill and bored a hole in the bow so that water could pour out. When the boat was dry, he plugged up the hole and slid the boat across the dam. Then the team reloaded and headed downriver.

This was quick thinking. Everyone remembered it, and when Abraham returned from New Orleans three months later, he had a new job. Denton Offutt made Lincoln the manager of his little store in New Salem. New Salem was happy to accept him. They welcomed him partly because families on the frontier were used to helping one another out. Their hard lives depended on trust and sharing.

Abraham surprised those he met. He looked like a bumpkin,

but when he spoke, people realized how smart he was. As the New Salem shoemaker said, "His appearance was od[d], but after all this bad appearance I soon found a very intelligent young man." Besides that, Abraham was hardworking, friendly, and funny. It wasn't long before he "knew every man, woman, & child for miles around."

Working at the store helped him meet people. So did boarding. In those days, young people far from home stayed and ate at neighbors' houses, paying a small fee, or doing chores like chopping wood or threshing wheat. Lincoln lived first at the store, sleeping among the crates and barrels. Then he boarded with different families, whose mothers took him under their wings. They cooked his meals, sewed his clothes, and did his washing.

He looked like a bumpkin, but when he spoke, people realized how smart he was.

What really sealed Lincoln's place in New Salem was his fight with Jack Armstrong. Jack was the leader of the Clary's Grove Boys, cousins from a village near the town. They were a rough

While living in New Salem, Abraham Lincoln resided in this rough-hewn home that was not unlike the log cabin he grew up in.

crew who usually made any newcomer to New Salem prove himself in a fight.

Everyone had a different account of Lincoln's contest with Armstrong. Some said that Denton Offutt boasted about his store clerk's strength, and before long, people were betting on a wrestling match between him and Jack Armstrong.

One afternoon, a ring of men gathered in front of Offutt's store to watch the show. Armstrong and Lincoln took hold of each other and started to wrestle. When Lincoln looked like he was going to win, Armstrong tried a dirty trick. Lincoln took it well and stood his ground. Some recalled that he offered to fight the whole gang, one by one.

Whatever actually happened, Lincoln's bravery and good humor won the day. Abraham and Jack walked away from the match as friends, and the Clary's Grove Boys liked the newcomer from then on.

A Learned Man

Older people in the town grew fond of Abraham, too. They liked his honesty and the fact that he didn't drink. They were amazed by his systematic efforts to teach himself. It seemed that he always had a book in his hand. He borrowed history, biography, and poetry books from the schoolmaster and from the tavern owner, James Rutledge. He borrowed law books and newspapers from the local justice of the peace, Bowling Green. People remembered seeing him reading as he walked, reading in between customers at the store, reading before work and after work.

Abraham's reading showed him that his backwoods grammar wasn't very good. He borrowed a grammar textbook and taught himself to read and write clearly and gracefully. His neighbors were surprised at how quickly he learned. "He read very thoroughly and had a most wonderful memory," said one. "[He] would distinctly remember almost everything he read."

The newspapers, law books, and talks with Bowling Green got Lincoln interested in government. In Illinois, the Whig and Democratic parties were beginning to form. Lincoln was a Whig. He believed in national unity and a national bank to help finance roads, railroads, and river transport. He opposed slavery and the expansion of it into new states. Senator Henry Clay of Kentucky, "The Great **Compromiser**," was one of his heroes.

A Born Leader

To put his beliefs into action, Lincoln decided in 1832, at the age of twenty-three, to run for the Illinois State Legislature. He announced that he was running and outlined his ideas in a letter to the local newspaper, the *Sangamo Journal*, but his campaign was cut short. The Native Americans in Illinois were becoming hostile and the U.S Army asked the state to raise a militia of volunteers to drive the tribes away. So New Salem formed its own company of seventy volunteers, including Lincoln.

In those days, militia companies elected their own officers. Someone nominated Lincoln, and to everyone's surprise, two-thirds of the men lined up behind him. Years later he said that the election was "a success which gave me more pleasure than any I have had since."

Lincoln often laughed about his military career. "I had a good many bloody struggles with the mosquitoes; and although I never fainted from loss of blood, I can truly say I was often very hungry," he said. Still, he reenlisted twice when his company's thirty-day service was over. In the end, the New

Henry Clay, "The Great Compromiser"

Lincoln admired the Kentuckian Henry Clay, who was a U.S. congressman, senator, and three-time candidate for president. He supported westward expansion and advocated the 1815 "American System" for building cross-countryroads, protecting manufacturers with high import taxes, and creating a national bank—the program that eventually became the Whig party **platform**.

The north and south were becoming increasingly divided on the issue of slavery and it was important that there be an equal number of free states and slave states, otherwise the balance of power might tip and those in the majority might try to overtake the country. Even though Clay was a slave owner, he did not want slavery to expand to new territories. Through his creation of the Missouri Compromise of 1820 and of 1850, Clay was able to maintain the balance between free states and slave states. In the Compromise of 1820, Maine entered as a free state to balance the slave state of Missouri. With the Compromise of 1850, California entered the **Union** as a free state and the New Mexico and Utah territories could choose to be slave or free.

This portrait of Henry Clay, "The Great Compromiser," hangs in the Capitol's Senate reception room.

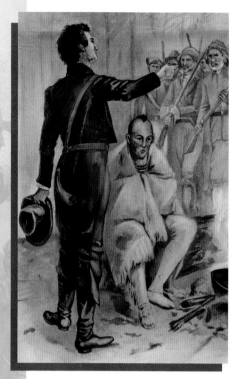

Abraham Lincoln of the Illinois militia is shown protecting an innocent tribesman from angry soldiers in this 19th-century lithograph.

Salem company never saw action against the hostile tribes. This war eventually came to be known as the Black Hawk War of 1832.

Abraham was pleased that he was leading people who would admire and support him for the rest of his life. "Lincoln was their idol," one soldier said, adding that "there was not a Man but was obedient to every word he spoke and would fight to the death for Lincoln." They admired him because "he Could out jump the Best of them he Could out Box the Best of them he Could Beat all of them on anecdote," another soldier remarked.

Lincoln was famous for his bravery as well. One day an elderly tribesman stumbled into his company's camp. Although the man had a certificate from U.S. authorities certifying that he was loyal to the British, the men wanted to shoot him anyway. Lincoln didn't hesitate. He shielded the terrified Indian. "Men, this must not be done," he said. "We must not shed his blood. It must not be on our shirts." The soldiers argued with him. They called him a coward. "If any man thinks I am a coward, let him test it," Lincoln replied. They said he was bigger and stronger than they were. "Choose your weapons, then," he said.

The men gave in, and the stranger went free. In the end, the men remembered the incident, and loved Lincoln for it.

The Black Hawk War of 1832

In 1804, as settlements expanded into western territories, the Sac and Fox tribes of Illinois were forced to cede fifty million acres of their land to the United States. Because of that loss, the tribes sided with the British in the War of 1812. Even after the war, clashes between Native Americans and settlers continued. The Native Americans were forced farther West, and the U.S. Army built a fort on Rock Island in Illinois, which was considered sacred to the tribes.

An 1833 painting by Charles Bird King pictures the Sac chief Black Hawk, who led an unsuccessful war against the United States in 1832.

While some of the tribes agreed to leave Illinois and signed a treaty promising to stay west of the Mississippi, a sixty-five-year-old Sac chief named Black Hawk led his people back into the state in the spring of 1832. Their goal was to plant their traditional spring wheat at Saukenuk—their name for Rock Island. Along the way, men of the Fox, Kickapoo, and Winnebago joined, and the group swelled to 2,000 people. But by August, Black Hawk's people were defeated. Most of them were killed by the U.S. Army.

CHAPTER 3

The Young Politician

My politics are short and sweet, like the old woman's dance.

Following the Black Hawk War, Abraham had a run of bad luck. He had lost the 1832 election for the Illinois State Legislature. His job disappeared when Denton

This illustration depicts Abe working in Denton Offutt's general store. Lincoln later bought his own store and had to repay a large sum, which he called the "National Debt."

Offutt's store closed and Offutt vanished. Abraham and a friend had opened a store, which failed and left Lincoln owing $1,100 to creditors. Lincoln called the huge sum the "National Debt." He swore to pay it off and did, bit by bit. This was one reason for his nickname, "Honest Abe."

Postmaster and Surveyor

In May 1833, Lincoln's luck changed. He may have lost the election, but his eloquent speeches had impressed his neighbors, even though most were Democrats and he was a Whig. Someone had persuaded the Democratic president, Andrew Jackson, to appoint Lincoln postmaster of New Salem, a job that paid him about twenty dollars a year and gave him the chance to read all the newspapers that came to the post office. With this small income and money from odd jobs like splitting rails, he scraped by.

A few months later there came a chance to learn another trade. People were pouring into Sangamon County, and its **surveyor**, John Calhoun, was swamped with work. Farmland, house sites, roads, and canals all had to be planned out. Calhoun had served with Lincoln in the Black Hawk War, and now he offered him the job of assistant surveyor. Very pleased, Lincoln accepted.

He taught himself so well that he became the local authority.

Abraham knew nothing about surveying, but he'd always been interested in math. He borrowed the standard surveying textbooks, and in a few months, taught himself all he needed to know about geometry and trigonometry and how to use them with surveying tools. He measured in dense forests, over hills, and across windy prairies, and then performed the calculations. As he did his rounds on his old horse, signs of his work hung all over him. His surveying compass, chains, and stakes poked out from his saddlebags; mail envelopes were stuck in

As a young man, Lincoln undertook many jobs. One was splitting rails, shown in this late 19th-century painting, by J. L. G. Ferris.

his hatband; and a book lay open on the saddle.

He taught himself so well that he became the local authority. One neighbor commented that when there were disputes among the settlers, Mr. Lincoln's compass and chain always settled the matter satisfactorily.

Surveying and delivering letters took Lincoln all around Sangamon County, and he often boarded with different people along the way. In doing so, he got to know many people, and he earned the respect of merchants, investors, and

As a surveyor, Lincoln used specific types of measuring equipment, such as the spirit level and graduated measurement rod, which are shown in this undated illustration.

politicians, many of them leaders of the large town of Springfield, twenty miles southeast of New Salem.

First Win in Politics

When the 1834 elections rolled around, Lincoln ran again for the state legislature. This time he had the backing of most of Sangamon County—both Democrats and Whigs—partly because voters knew he believed in building transportation networks, which the county desperately needed. He also had the backing of men who had marched with him in the Black Hawk War, noticed him in his 1832 campaign, and observed his work ethic. Among them were two prominent lawyers, John Todd Stuart, the head of

The Whigs and Democrats

The presidency of Andrew Jackson (1829–1837) brought a new set of political parties. With his supporters, Jackson created the Democratic Party, which was later opposed by the Whigs, the party of Lincoln's choice.

The Democrats included small farmers, craftsmen, laborers, and Irish and German immigrants. They were for the old-fashioned farming life, with independence and the least possible government. They feared the new market economy and disliked the **tariffs**—import taxes—that protected Northern industry. They were against state and national banks, which they believed gave wealth to a few rich people. On the question of slavery, the party was split, North against South.

The Whigs, named for an old English party, were progressive doctors, lawyers, and businessmen. They believed in personal meaning public works like railroads, highways, and canals. They supported state banks to help fund these improvements and high tariffs to protect businesses. Most were antislavery, ranging in intensity from **abolitionists** to moderate reformers.

one of the first families to settle in Springfield, and Stephen J. Logan, who said of Lincoln, "He was a very tall, gawky, and rough-looking fellow then....But after he began speaking I became very much interested in him. He made a very sensible speech."

Most important, John Todd Stuart noticed Lincoln. Stuart was a college-educated Springfield lawyer and a state representative. He had served with Lincoln in the militia. In fact, the two young men had come home from far-off Wisconsin together, walking most of the way. Stuart urged Abraham to study law, and he lent him classic law textbooks.

Most lawyers at the time either learned law in college or studied with older attorneys. Lincoln had no money for college, and there were no attorneys in New Salem, so he studied on his own.

Busy with studying, delivering mail, and surveying, Lincoln did little campaigning in 1834. His speeches were straightforward: "My politics are short and sweet, like the old woman's dance. I am in favor of a national bank. I am in favor of the internal improvement system and a high protective tariff. These are my sentiments and political principles. If elected, I shall be thankful; if not, it will be all the same."

He was learning. But he was already useful to his party because of his writing, which was clear and logical.

People paid attention because, as a fellow Whig put it, "of the standing he had got in the country, and especially the prominence given him by his captaincy in the Black Hawk War—because he was a good fellow—because he told good stories, and remembered good jokes—because he was genial, kind, sympathetic, open-hearted—because when he was asked a question and gave an answer it was always characteristic, brief, pointed, apropos, out of the common way and manner, and yet exactly suited to the time and place and thing. . . . "

Lincoln easily won the election. Among the first things he did upon winning was visit a rich farmer named Coleman Smoot. He asked Smoot if he had voted for him. When Smoot replied that he had, Abraham asked him to "loan me money to buy Suitable Clothing for I want to make a decent appearance in the Legislature."

Smoot loaned him $200, which Lincoln repaid as promised.

So in December, wearing a new suit, Lincoln rode a stagecoach ninety-five miles across the icy Illinois prairie to Vandalia, a frontier town of 800 people living in log cabins. Its statehouse was built of brick, but it was falling apart. The legislators worked inside the dimly lit hallways, while covered wagons bumped along the muddy streets outside day after day as pioneers headed West.

Abraham roomed with John Todd Stuart above a tavern. Stuart, the Whig floor leader, was responsible for organizing his party's strategy. But he also taught Abraham the ins and outs of politics. In that first session of the Legislature, Lincoln mostly listened. He was learning. But he was already useful to his party because of his writing, which was clear and logical. He wrote bills and **resolutions** for the Whigs.

The tavern in New Salem where Lincoln met his beloved Ann Rutledge is shown in this 1950 photograph.

Ann Rutledge

Ann Rutledge was the daughter of James Rutledge, one of the founders of New Salem, and Lincoln probably met her when he boarded at the family tavern. At that time, Ann was engaged to a merchant named John McNamar. But McNamar went back to his home in New York to visit his family in 1832. He never wrote to Ann, which allowed Lincoln the opportunity to court her. In February 1835, after Lincoln's first legislative session was over, they became engaged.

Ann insisted on a secret engagement because she felt it was not honorable to marry until she had a chance to inform the missing McNamar. Then, during one of the hottest and wettest Augusts in Illinois history, she fell victim to "brain fever," which was probably typhoid. Lincoln was a constant visitor, but on August 25, the bright, kindly, golden-haired Ann Rutledge died.

Lincoln's first love, Ann Rutledge, is buried at this gravesite in Petersburg, Illinois

Love and No Marriage

Abraham felt very happy. People liked him. He was on the road to seeing his dreams come true. And he was in love with the prettiest girl in New Salem. Her name was Ann Rutledge, and they planned to marry. Unfortunately, Ann died unexpectedly during what might have been an epidemic of typhoid. Lincoln, who usually hid his deepest feelings under a genial mask, despaired. He grew thin and avoided even his closest friends, who began to fear for his sanity. Some thought he might even kill himself. Some, who didn't know about his engagement, thought he had tired himself out studying law.

Abraham's landlady, Elizabeth Abell, said she had never seen a man mourn more for a companion. Old Bowling Green, the justice of the peace who'd lent Lincoln books,

"I have now come to the conclusion never again to think of marrying."

stepped in to help. He took Abraham to his own home and took care of him for weeks, until he felt able to get on with his studies and his work.

Late the next year, Mrs. Abell suggested to Abraham that he might like to marry her sister Mary Owen. Lincoln met Mary, who had come from a good Kentucky family and who was bright and pretty. He agreed and said he "saw no good objection to plodding life through hand in hand with her."

Mrs. Abell brought Mary back to New Salem, but in Lincoln's eyes, Mary had grown heavy and unattractive. As for Mary, she found Lincoln moody and bad mannered. Perhaps he was still mourning Ann. Since he had given his word to marry her, he proposed, but in such a reluctant way that Mary turned him down.

His vanity was hurt. He'd made a fool of himself, he thought. "I have now come to the conclusion never again to think of marrying," he wrote, "and for this reason: I can never be satisfied with anyone who would be blockhead enough to have me."

But he would prove himself wrong.

CHAPTER 4

A Springfield Romance

I am quite as lonesome here as I ever was anywhere in my life.

The year 1837 was a full one for Abraham Lincoln. He'd passed his law exams, recieved his liscense, and joined John Todd Stuart's law firm. He'd also been reelected to the state legislature. He moved to Springfield, the new capital of Illinois. Springfield was booming even though parts of the city had hogs, horses, and cows wandering through the dirt streets, which turned into mud in wet weather. When it was hot, prairie fires blazed and the air smelled of smoke, animals, and outhouses.

Still, the new state capital seemed sophisticated after New Salem. Springfield's two thousand citizens had churches, private schools, and a lyceum—a club where people heard lectures. Distinguished families of the town lived in handsome houses that stood in an area called "Aristocrat's Hill." These families included the Edwardses, Todds, and Stuarts.

One April Saturday when Abraham stopped at a general store

Civil War photographer Mathew Brady took this portrait of Joshua Speed—one of Lincoln's closest and most loyal friends.

to buy some bed linens, Joshua Speed, part owner of the store, thought, "I never saw a sadder face." Speed had a generous heart, and Lincoln's sadness touched him. He said that he had a large room above the store that Lincoln was welcome to share. Abraham carried his saddlebags up the stairs. When he came down, Speed had to laugh. Lincoln was beaming happily. "Well, Speed, I am moved," he said. That meeting began the closest friendship of Abraham's life. Joshua Speed was twenty-three to Abraham's twenty-eight. Unlike Lincoln, Speed was a handsome, well-educated young man from a grand and loving family.

A Friendly Gathering Place

Although Lincoln and Speed came from different backgrounds, the two shared many things. They loved poetry and talked about it for hours. Lincoln's favorites were William Shakespeare and Robert Burns. Speed admired Lord Byron. They both wanted wives, which they also discussed for hours, and they were both Whigs.

Like this country store gathering, Joshua Speed's general store quickly became a gathering place for political discussions and Lincoln's entertaining stories.

The new Illinois State House, pictured in this 1858 engraving, is where Lincoln served three out of his four terms as a state legislator.

Often they would talk long into the evenings. Speed's store quickly became a clubhouse for young Springfield lawyers. As Joshua remembered about Lincoln, "After he made his home with me, on every winter's night at my store, by a big wood fire, no matter how inclement the weather, eight or ten choice spirits assembled, without distinction of party."

They came for poetry, for Abraham's stories, and for politics. One topic favored by the Whigs was internal improvement. Improvements were popular in booming Illinois; in fact, in January, Lincoln had helped push through a 10 million-dollar bill for constructing roads, railroads, and canals. The Whigs had also helped create the Illinois State Bank to finance the projects.

Another lively topic around the fire was party organization. Until the mid-1830s, politics in Illinois were local, personal, and not too **partisan.** For instance, many Democratic friends voted for Lincoln in 1834 and 1836.

But then the Democrats organized their party nationally. When Illinois Whigs saw how this won elections, they formed a Central Committee, with Lincoln a key member. He divided each Illinois county into voting districts led by locals who could encourage people to vote.

The Issue of Slavery

The most contentious political topic that was heating up everywhere was slavery. **Abolitionists** called for its end, enraging Southern slaveholders. Even though Illinois was a free state, the people were still antiabolitionist and anti-black. The few free blacks who lived there could not legally vote, sit on juries, or even go to school, but they did have to pay taxes.

In this atmosphere, it's not surprising that in early 1837, the Illinois legislature adopted some resolutions from Southern states that announced Southerners had the "sacred" right to own slaves. They also called abolitionists an evil threat to the Union.

An 1835 engraving of an anti-slavery meeting in Boston shows a few free blacks in attendance.

Of the eighty-three Illinois representatives, seventy-seven voted for the resolutions. Lincoln led the six who voted against them. Then Lincoln and another legislator entered a protest on the record. They wanted to show their hatred of slavery. They also wanted to make it clear that they were not abolitionists, because being known as an abolitionist in Illinois could ruin one's political career. Ultimately, Lincoln believed that slavery was wrong but that it was protected by the U.S. Constitution. In fact, the Constitution—some of whose framers were slave owners— regulated slavery in three ways. First, under the subject of

Abolitionists

By the early nineteenth century, America was home to four million African slaves. Thanks to early reformers, slavery was illegal in Northern states, but the South's economy depended on the slaves.

The slaves' wretched lives inspired an abolitionist movement—a movement demanding that slavery be abolished immediately, whatever the law, and whatever the cost to the Union. It was led by New York editor William Lloyd Garrison and the former slave Frederick Douglass, among others. To them, slavery was a terrible evil and slave owners vile sinners.

In 1833, abolitionists organized the American Antislavery Society. Its members **lobbied**, petitioned Congress, and exposed the horrors of slavery in newspapers, books, and sermons. Also many abolitionists supported the Underground Railroad, a secret network that helped slaves to freedom. Some extremists called for violence to free the slaves.

Southern slaveholders were outraged. They answered with their own violent speeches and newspaper articles. They also passed harsh state laws protecting slavery. But moderate, antislavery Northerners were also

apportionment, it stated that in determining a state's population, each slave would count as three-fifths of a person. (Slaves, of course, could not vote.) Then it said that Congress could not prohibit the slave trade until 1808. Finally, the Constitution said that a slave who escaped to a free state did not become free; instead, the slave had to be returned to his owner.

Lincoln revered the Constitution, believing that its laws must be obeyed until they could be changed, but he could protest against resolutions glorifying human bondage. The protest, his first public comment on the subject, refused to call slavery a

Many abolitionists aided the Underground Railroad (depicted in this 1893 painting), which secretly helped slaves escape to freedom.

worried about abolitionists. Many of these Northerners were racists who feared that freed slaves would migrate north. They also feared that extreme abolitionist preaching would drive Southerners to violence or even to war. They were right. Only after a war, two presidential proclamations, and a Constitutional amendment did American slavery finally come to an end. Abolitionists played a large part in making it happen.

"sacred" right and abolition a sin. It said, instead, "that the institution of slavery is founded on both injustice and bad policy; but that the **promulgation** of abolition doctrines tends rather to increase its evils." Through his well-crafted eloquence, he was able to present a cool overview of a hot situation.

In a speech given at Springfield's Young Men's Lyceum in January 1838, Lincoln stated his belief in the great American system of government, but warned that it was "an undecided experiment." He said that "when the vicious portion of population shall be permitted to gather in bands of hundreds and thousands, and burn churches…. throw printing presses into rivers, shoot editors…. with impunity; depend on it, this Government cannot last." He pleaded for cool reason.

Like many early speeches, this one was fashionably ornate. Lincoln was still finding his own style, in this and other things. For instance, while he was a kind man, he could be cruel in political conflict. Like other politicians, too, Lincoln wrote anonymous newspaper articles that at times were nasty—and slanderous.

A Stormy Courtship

Although Lincoln was beginning to find his place in politics and in his work, social acceptance came slowly. "I am as lonesome here as I ever was anywhere in my life," he wrote. He may have heard about the parties and balls, picnics and taffy pulls on Aristocrat's Hill, but at first he wasn't invited. As one person remarked, "Lincoln, although an extremely clever and

Although Lincoln was beginning to find his place in politics and in his work, social acceptance came slowly.

well-liked fellow, was hardly up to our standard of gentility."

It was true. Abraham's poor background showed in his manners and speech. But rising men could not be ignored, and besides, Lincoln had cultivated friends like Joshua Speed and John Todd Stuart. They introduced him to the house of Stuart's cousins, Ninian and Elizabeth Edwards, leaders of Springfield society.

Lincoln spent most of the year speaking at rallies around Illinois and helped create "the rowdiest, noisiest presidential campaign in the history of the country."

There, in late 1839, Abraham met Elizabeth's sister, Mary Ann Todd, of Lexington. The daughter of a Whig banker, Mary was a plump, pretty little woman of twenty-one. She was well educated, fashionable, and flirtatious. She loved poetry. Unlike most women, she was interested in politics—a "violent little Whig," a relative had called her.

Soon Abraham became enchanted with the lovely Miss Todd. Elizabeth Edwards, who thought Lincoln lower class, noted disapprovingly that she often found the pair together. When Mary spoke, Elizabeth said, "Lincoln would gaze on her as if drawn by some superior power, irresistibly so."

The friendship grew during the presidential race of 1840, when Lincoln campaigned for Whig William Henry Harrison and his vice president, John Tyler.

Lincoln spent most of the year speaking at rallies around Illinois and helped create "the rowdiest, noisiest presidential campaign in the history of the country." At some point he wrote to Mary, and she replied. She said he was "the most congenial mind she had ever met." Some thought they were engaged to be married.

But Lincoln had a change of heart, and when he returned to Springfield in the fall, he told Mary he didn't love her. Some speculated that he was afraid of marriage. Others believed he fell in love with Mary's beautiful young cousin. Wounded, Mary told him to go.

By January, Abraham's spirit was broken. He was exhausted from months on the road—and while Harrison won the national contest, he did not win in Illinois, despite Lincoln's

This photograph of Mary Todd Lincoln was taken c. 1846. Unlike most of the women of her time, Mary was very interested in political matters and supported the Whig party.

hard work. The Whigs' expensive improvements were pushing Illinois toward bankruptcy, and it was endangering Lincoln's political career.

His best friend, Joshua, was moving home to Kentucky. And Abraham felt terrible about Mary. He worried about his own lack of resolution and about his honor. As a result he couldn't sleep, eat, or work. He despaired. "To remain as I am is impossible," he wrote. "I must die or be better." Fearing what Abraham might do, Joshua removed the razors from Lincoln's room.

After a week passed, a pale and gaunt Abraham dragged himself back for his last session in the legislature. He and Stuart amicably broke up their firm, and Lincoln joined a new partner, another Todd cousin, Stephen J. Logan.

Abraham felt terrible about Mary. He worried about his own lack of resolution and about his honor. As a result he couldn't sleep, eat, or work.

Then, in August of 1841, Lincoln visited Joshua at the Speed family's Kentucky plantation. Speed was in love with a pretty neighbor named Fanny Henning and he felt most anxious about it. For months afterword, Abraham wrote Joshua letters full of sympathetic advice. He knew what his friend was going through. He still thought about Mary, whom he had treated badly. Her sadness, he wrote, "kills my soul."

When Speed married in 1842 and wrote about his happiness, Lincoln thought of his own. That year, Abraham and Mary were reunited. At the same time, Mary Todd wrote some anonymous letters in the *Sangamo Journal* with her friend, Julia Jayne. In the letters, they called the Democratic state auditor, James Shields, "a liar as well as a fool." Shields demanded the names of the writers, and Lincoln offered to protect the women

The Illinois marriage certificate of Abraham and Mary Todd Lincoln clearly shows the date of their marriage—November 4, 1842.

by taking the blame. When Shields learned that it was Lincoln who was behind the letters, he challenged him to a duel.

Even though dueling was illegal in Illinois and Abraham despised violence, no politician could afford to be seen as a coward, so Lincoln accepted the challenge. He chose the weapons—cavalry broadswords, which gave a tall man an advantage—and he practiced.

The duelists and their seconds or dueling assistants traveled to Missouri, where dueling was legal, but there was no duel. Their seconds settled the quarrel instead with explanations and apologies. Lincoln was so ashamed of himself that he never talked about the affair again. He also stopped writing anonymous articles.

Soon after this, Lincoln did what he believed was the honorable thing and proposed to Mary. They were married on November 4, 1842. Lincoln gave Mary a wedding ring inscribed "Love Is Eternal."

CHAPTER 5

Mr. Lincoln Goes to Congress

[I want] to link [my] name with something that would redound to the interest of [my] fellow man.

In 1844, Lincoln campaigned for Henry Clay, who was running for president against James K. Polk. Despite his efforts, Clay lost the election. When he finished his work, he returned to Indiana to look again at the country around Little Pigeon Creek. It was the summertime of 1844 and Abraham rode along dirt roads through the scenes of his childhood. He walked the fields where he'd worked so hard as a boy, remembering his mother and his sister, who had both died at Little Pidgeon Creek. Time changed everything, he thought sadly.

As a young man, Lincoln may have suffered from depression. This somber photograph of him was taken when he was about 35 years old.

Lincoln, the Poet

Lincoln, the great statesman, was also a sensitive poet, who put down on paper his innermost feelings. There are poems that he wrote even in childhood, and many of his poems reflect a great melancholy. When he returned to Pigeon Creek in 1844, he wrote "My Childhood's Home I See Again."

...Near twenty years have passed away
Since here I bid farewell
To woods and fields, and scenes of play,
And playmates loved so well.

Where many were, how few remain
Of old familiar things;
But seeing them, to mind again
The lost and absent brings.

The friends I left that parting day,
How changed, as time has sped!
Young childhood grown, strong manhood gray,
And half of all are dead....

At thirty-five, Abraham had become a sad man and may have suffered from chronic depression. Everyone who knew him saw this. He had, a lawyer friend wrote, "a settled form of melancholy, sometimes very marked, and sometimes very mild, but always sufficient to tinge his countenance with a shade of sadness, unless a smile should dispel it, which frequently happened." He used his famous sense of humor, a longtime colleague said, "to whistle off sadness."

Several things helped Lincoln out of his depression. One

was his decision to marry Mary Todd. When Abraham decided to marry Mary Todd, he felt he had done the honorable thing and had restored what he called "the gem" of his character—his ability to keep to his decisions.

Another was his ambition. He said to his friend Joshua Speed that he wanted to be part of the great events of his time. He wanted "to link his name with something that would redound to the interest of his fellow man."

He thought it was his destiny to do something for his nation. He deeply believed in American government, founded on the Declaration of Independence—a holy document, to Lincoln—and the Constitution. While he waited to see how his future would play out, he threw himself into his work, one of his best defenses against sadness.

He deeply believed in American government, founded on the Declaration of Independence.

Hostile Political Times

Even though Lincoln seemed to have suffered from depression, he had come a long way from his barefoot Indiana beginnings. He was a successful lawyer. He had finally paid off the old "National Debt" from his New Salem years. He and Mary Todd had bought a comfortable house at Eighth and Jackson Streets in Springfield, and they had a one-year-old son, Robert.

Lincoln was also an important Illinois Whig. He no longer held office in the state legislature but was busy on Whig committees and helped shape campaigns and policies. In just a couple of years he would step into a political world that was becoming ever more hostile day by day, thanks to the political battles between Southerners, who wanted new slave states, and

Northerners, who wanted free states. With the death of President William Henry Harrison after only one month in office, the balance of slave and free states was in jeopardy again. The Republic of Texas, a territory that had **seceded** from Mexico, wanted to join the United States as a slave state. The political wrangling around this territory ultimately led to war with Mexico in 1846.

The Mexican War

In 1844, James Polk, promising to annex Texas, won the presidency. Then, in 1845, Congress passed a resolution admitting Texas into the Union as a slave state, but the borders of Texas and Mexico were in dispute. When Mexico sent troops to the Rio Grande River, Polk sent the U.S. Army to protect the southern border of Texas and to keep the Mexican army from crossing the river. Both the annexation and the U.S. Army troops were provocations to Mexico, which still claimed Texas as its own. So Mexican troops attacked the Americans in the spring of 1846. In response, Congress declared war.

When the war ended in 1848, Mexico **ceded** the territories of New Mexico and California to the United States. Now the U.S borders stretched all the way to the Pacific Ocean.

This 1847 lithograph depicts the Battle of Buena Vista during the Mexican-American War. Mexico's eventual defeat led to their cession of large expanses of land to the United States.

A pro-Democrat political cartoon of 1844 shows James K. Polk (holding the American flag) competing with the Whigs and Henry Clay (sitting in the river) over the annexation of Texas.

That year, Abraham Lincoln ran for the U.S. Congress in the midst of a war frenzy. Some Americans thought it was America's right to turn Southwestern land into U.S. states. Some, of course, saw a chance to add slave states to the Union.

Whigs wanted no new slave states. In Congress, Whigs tried to get control. When President Polk asked for money for negotiations with Mexico, Representative David Wilmot of Pennsylvania added a **proviso** saying that there could be no slavery in any territory taken from Mexico. The House passed the bill. The Southern-controlled Senate did not.

Lincoln the Congressman

While the military battles in the Southwest and the political battles in Congress raged on, Abraham Lincoln easily won his congressional seat. By the autumn of 1847, when he moved to Washington, the Whigs' position was clear. They wanted to

During the 1846 elections, the Whig party passed out handbills that listed the party's ticket. At the top of the list was Abraham Lincoln for Congress.

disgrace Polk for starting an unnecessary war of conquest, and they were determined to put a Whig in the White House in the 1848 elections.

The Lincolns—Abraham, Mary, Rob, and the new baby Eddie, born in 1846— arrived in Washington in the chill November of 1847. It had been a long, difficult trip by stagecoach, steamboat, and train from Springfield. Life in Washington was very different from the comfortable elegance of Mary's childhood in Lexington. The city was set in a former swamp, and it was only partly built. The Capitol had a temporary wooden dome. Most streets were unpaved and, as in Springfield, were cluttered with horses, stray dogs, and hogs. The little family took a room in Mrs. Spriggs's boarding house, which was near the Capitol, where the Library of Congress stands today.

Upon settling in Washington, Abraham got to work. As for Mary, she was miserable even though she liked the city's shops and theaters and enjoyed the parties she attended. Of the ten congressmen boarding with Mrs. Spriggs, only Lincoln had brought his wife.

Edward (Eddie) Baker Lincoln was born in 1846 and was the second son of Abraham and Mary Lincoln.

When the Lincolns first arrived in Washington, D.C., they must have seen the Capitol as it appeared in this photograph, c. 1846.

She didn't care for some of the other boarders, and they didn't like her. The weather was damp and nasty and little Eddie was sickly. Abraham was always busy. In the spring, she took the children back to her father's house in Lexington.

Now alone and often lonely, the freshman congressman from Illinois spent his time learning the ropes. He served on committees; tried to get patents, favors, and public offices for his Illinois supporters; and made speeches for the Whig program.

His major speeches were part of the Whig attack on President Polk. In them he accused Polk of lying about how the

Mexican War started. He demanded repeatedly to know the exact "spot" where American blood had first been shed, claiming it was on Mexican soil. Polk, he said, had started the war on purpose. Now he couldn't end it.

President Polk ignored the speech. Democrats in Congress ridiculed it. Democrats at home in Illinois called Lincoln a traitor for questioning the war and dubbed him "Spotty Lincoln." And unfortunately for Lincoln, Mexico signed a peace treaty two weeks after his speech, ceding most of its North American territory, which eventually became the states of the American Southwest.

It wasn't Abraham's finest hour, but he soldiered on. He threw himself into the Whigs' new presidential campaign—for the Mexican war hero Zachary Taylor, who they thought was the one man who could win.

The Slavery Debate Rages On

Taylor did win, and after the campaigning was over, Lincoln returned for his second and final session of Congress. He wasn't going to run again. The Illinois Whigs had an agreement about rotating their congressional candidates, and he had had his turn.

Because of the Mexican War, it was a

This 1847 engraving is of Zachary Taylor, hero of the Mexican War and successful Whig candidate for the 1848 presidential election.

session of shouting, resolutions and counterresolutions, threats and counterthreats in both the House and the Senate. Antislavery Northerners vowed to keep slavery out of the new territories. Southerners argued that they could extend federal laws protecting slavery all the way to California, making a slave empire. Lincoln was disgusted by the violent speeches and the threats thrown around by lawmakers. But mostly he was horrified by the danger to the Union growing before his eyes.

Lincoln was disgusted by the violent speeches and the threats thrown around by lawmakers. But mostly he was horrified by the danger to the Union growing before his eyes.

After some uncertainty about how to approach the issue, Lincoln, in January of 1849, announced that he would introduce a bill to abolish slavery in the District of Columbia, gradually, with payment to their owners. This enraged Southerners. Lincoln's plan also included a rule that escaped slaves in Washington would have to be sent back to their owners. This infuriated Northerners.

Neither side supported him, and Lincoln never presented the bill. He heard with despair the reaction of the South Carolina Senator John C. Calhoun, who said that if slaves were **emancipated**, the white race would be destroyed. The blacks would unite with Northerners, destroying the Southern way of life. Calhoun said that if Southerners united behind white supremacy, the North would see the danger and become more reasonable. Calhoun's ugly threat of Southern secession was very clear.

CHAPTER 6

The Illinois Lawyer

*He was the great big man of our firm,
and I was the little one.*

—William Herndon

When Lincoln's congressional term ended, he went home
to Illinois to concentrate on his law practice. For a
man who'd lived all his life in log cabins or rented rooms,
Lincoln's house at Eighth and Jackson Streets in
Springfield was a sign of success. It was built of clapboard

Lincoln's home in Springfield, Illinois, is shown in this undated photograph.
The house was a sign of Lincoln's success and was a far cry from the
dilapidated log cabins of his youth.

painted a fashionable brown. Inside was a central hall with double parlors, and upstairs, four bedrooms. The kitchen was in the back near the pump—for well water—and the woodshed, where Abraham chopped logs for the stoves that heated the house. A privy, or outdoor toilet, stood behind the shed, and behind that lay a field where the Lincolns' horse and milk cow grazed.

Wherever Lincoln went, he often wore his favorite black stovepipe hat. Typically, similar hats of that era were fashioned from a stiff felt that was made from matted beaver fur.

The house was the family's home base from 1849 to 1861, years when—although the dangers to the nation were often in his mind—Lincoln stayed out of political office to build his law practice. Every morning he'd feed and curry his horse and eat breakfast with Mary and the boys. Then, he'd walk the few blocks to his office, a tall, thin, stooped man wearing his ubiquitous stovepipe hat.

Lincoln's Law Practice

The office Lincoln shared with his new partner, William Herndon, was in Springfield's Courthouse Square. Its two dingy rooms were furnished with a desk, a sofa, a chair, and a bearskin rug. The office was usually a mess, with fruit peelings on the floor, and books and papers everywhere. There was even a bundle of papers on the desk with a sign in Lincoln's writing: "If you can't find it anywhere, look in here."

The two partners were very different. Herndon, nine years

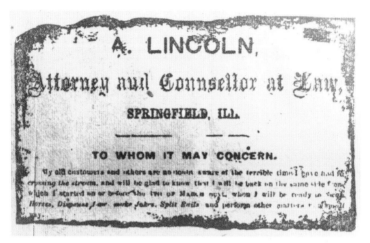

A. LINCOLN,

Attorney and Counsellor at Law,

SPRINGFIELD, ILL.

TO WHOM IT MAY CONCERN.

My old customers and others are no doubt aware of the terrible time I have had in crossing the stream, and will be glad to know that I am back on the same side from which I started on or before the 1st of March next, when I will be ready to Swap Horses, Dispense Law, make Jokes, Split Rails and perform other old tricks at short notice.

When Lincoln returned to Springfield, he passed out business cards to let people know he was practicing law again. The bold letters read "A. Lincoln, Attorney and Counsellor at Law."

younger than Lincoln, was an emotional man who believed more in intuition than logic. He was a great reader, always bubbling over about the latest books. In politics he was "somewhat of a radical," as he said himself, with close ties to abolitionist groups.

Herndon idolized the cool, rational Lincoln, whom he'd known for years. In fact, it was Abraham who suggested that Herndon study law, and Lincoln who surprised him with the offer of a partnership. "He was the great big man of our firm, and I was the little one," Herndon would later say. "The little one naturally looked up to the big one."

Lincoln called him Billy. Herndon called his partner Mr. Lincoln, or Lincoln. So did most of Lincoln's friends. A few called him Abraham. Nobody called him Abe, at least not to his face. He hated the nickname.

As different as they were, the partners got along well. Yet Herndon, who studied the man closely for sixteen years, never felt that he really understood Lincoln. He spoke for most of Abraham's friends when he later wrote that Lincoln "was the most reticent and mostly secretive man that ever existed: he never opened his whole soul to any man: he never touched the history or quality of his own nature in the presence of his friends." The open young fellow of the New Salem years had become a man who never talked about himself.

Still, Herndon and Lincoln built a prosperous law practice. They took every kind of case: divorce, disputed wills, debts, slander suits, and criminal cases. They took many patent cases, which fascinated Lincoln. And during the railroad-building 1850s, they became known as railroad lawyers. Lincoln tried at least 240 cases before the Illinois Supreme Court. With his careful preparation—helped by Billy's research—his clarity, and his logic, he won most of them. Other lawyers admired him.

This 1869 photograph shows the street in Springfield where Abraham Lincoln and William Herndon's law office was located.

Lincoln's McCormick vs. Manny Case

Not unlike today, people of Lincoln's era judged a person by his appearance, and this was especially true if you were a lawyer. In 1854, Cyrus McCormick, inventor of the reaper, sued John H. Manny of Illinois for infringing on one of his patents. Both sides hired top lawyers. Manny's were legal stars—Peter H. Watson of Washington and George Harding of Philadelphia. But they wanted a third partner who was local and known to the judge. Someone recommended Lincoln, and Watson traveled to Springfield to meet him.

Not impressed, Watson thought Lincoln's house was too humble and considered the lanky gentleman crude, provincial, and odd looking. But Lincoln was intelligent, and Watson didn't want to offend the locals, so he offered Lincoln the case. When Watson returned home and described Lincoln to Harding, the men decided to hire another lawyer without telling Abraham. They did not even send Lincoln the court papers or testimony that were needed. But Abraham went to work anyway, carefully preparing his argument, or brief.

Only half of Lincoln's cases were tried in Springfield. The rest he argued at the scattered sites of the Eighth Illinois **Circuit Court**. Twice a year, Presiding Judge David Davis would travel to fourteen Illinois counties—covering more than 400 miles— to hear cases in remote settlements. With him rode such attorneys as the famous criminal lawyer Leonard Swett; Jesse Fell, who started an important Whig newspaper; and the entertaining (and often drunk) Ward Hill Laymon. Of all the crew, only Lincoln rode the entire circuit, three months in the spring and three in the fall.

No one told Abraham that the trial had been moved to Cincinnati, Ohio, but he found out about it. When he showed up in Cincinnati and met Harding and the preferred new lawyer, Edwin M. Stanton of Pittsburgh, they barely spoke to the "backwoodsman."

When Lincoln was forced to withdraw from the case, he offered Harding the brief he had so carefully written, but Harding never even read it. Lincoln stayed on to learn how the great lawyers made their case. But the two lawyers ignored him. Harding and Stanton eventually won the case, and Lincoln was ultimately paid $2,000 for "his services."

This is an 1865 engraving of Edwin Stanton, who eventually became one of Lincoln's trusted cabinet members.

The judge and the lawyer became friends. They slept in run-down taverns, twenty to a room. After court closed, they gathered around the tavern fireplaces, talking law and politics. Despite hardships like bad weather and bad food, Lincoln enjoyed the circuit. Judge Davis said, "I think Mr. Lincoln was happy—as happy as he could be, when on this circuit, and happy no other place. This was his place of enjoyment. As a general rule when all the lawyers of a Saturday evening would go home and see their families & friends at home Lincoln would refuse to go home." Davis was hinting at rumors about Lincoln's

unhappy married life. The judge didn't much care for
Mary Lincoln. He thought she was a snob with an
unladylike interest in politics.

Life with Mary Todd Lincoln

Mary Lincoln was a complicated woman. She had
come from a grand Kentucky family and had grown up
being waited on by slaves. She had a good education, was
quick witted and lively, and
she had had many admirers
before she fell in love with
Abraham. None of this had
prepared her for the life of a
middle-class housewife in the
mid-nineteenth century.

A housewife was
supposed to provide a quiet,
smoothly run home, a haven

*"Her table was famed for
the excellence of its rare
Kentucky dishes and in
season was loaded with
venison, wild turkeys,
prairie chickens and quail
and other game."*

for her husband. But creating a haven wasn't easy. All the
water for the house had to be pumped, the stove stoked,
the food cooked, and the insects killed, for there were no
window screens. A good wife was also supposed to create
dinner parties and teas. Mary loved parties, and here is
where she excelled. "Her table was famed for the
excellence of its rare Kentucky dishes and in season was
loaded with venison, wild turkeys, prairie chickens and
quail and other game," wrote Chicago lawyer Isaac
Arnold, one of her many guests.

Mrs. Lincoln also loved the other part of the wife's
job—being a mother. By 1850, Bobby was seven and

Edward was four. Eddie had always been sickly and that year, after a death struggle of two months, he died of tuberculosis. Abraham wept, but Mary became completely despondent. She kept to her room for weeks, and only Abraham could persuade her to the table. "Eat, Mary, for we must live," he'd say.

A year later, another son, William, was born, and this comforted both Lincolns. Their last son, Thomas (called Tad because he had a large head like a tadpole) arrived in 1853.

Mary Todd Lincoln (photographed here between 1855 and 1865) presented the image of a model wife, who excelled at social entertaining.

Both Lincolns spoiled the boys. Everyone talked about it. The "little devils" drove Billy Herndon crazy at the office. He said they "would take down the books—empty ash buckets—coal ashes—inkstands—papers—gold pens—letters etc. etc., in a pile and then dance on the pile." Lincoln would just laugh.

However, it wasn't the children who gave Mary her difficult reputation. She had a terrible temper and had more trouble than most keeping housemaids. She screamed at them and sometimes even slapped them. "She always talked to us as if we had no feelings, and I was never so unhappy in my life as while living with her," said one ex-maid.

An 1861 painting by Francis Carpenter shows Mary and Abraham Lincoln with their three sons, Robert, William, and Thomas (also called Tad). Their second son, Edward, had died in 1850.

She screamed at Abraham, too, and sometimes she threw books at him. Lincoln kept the kind of cool control he always showed. Kind and polite himself, he ignored Mary's tantrums. "Lincoln & his wife got along tolerably well, unless Mrs. L. got the devil in her," said a neighbor. "Lincoln paid no attention—would pick up one of his children & walked off...."

Despite her fury, Mary loved and admired Abraham and she took very good care of him. She thought he could do anything. Often times she would harp and snap at him in order to correct his clothes and manners, for she believed, well before the thought crossed anyone's mind, that one day Abraham Lincoln could be president of the United States.

CHAPTER 7

The Great Slavery Debates

A house divided against itself cannot stand.

In 1854, Abraham Lincoln was still practicing law in Springfield, but events surrounding the issue of slavery propelled him back into the political world. It was the year that Illinois Senator Stephen Douglas set off a firestorm by sponsoring the Kansas-Nebraska Act. If the act passed, the vast Nebraska Territory—most of the northern part of the Louisiana Purchase—would be organized into two new states and would, no doubt, serve the Senator's personal business interests.

A map shows the Kansas and Nebraska Territories as they were drawn in 1854.

To get enough votes for his act in the Senate, Douglas needed the support of at least six Southern senators, but no Southerners would vote for a bill that would create more non-slave states. In order to get his Southern votes, Douglas included language in his act that would repeal the Missouri Compromise allowing citizens in each territory to choose whether to have slaves or not. He called this "popular **sovereignty**."

Both antislavery Whigs and Democrats were horrified. The act removed all legal restrictions against the spread of slavery.

Both antislavery Whigs and Democrats were horrified. The act removed all legal restrictions against the spread of slavery. Each party split within, so that it was North against South. Nevertheless, amid violent scenes of shouting, fistfights, and drawn weapons, Congress made the bill law on May 30, 1854.

Speaking Out Against Slavery

Abraham Lincoln was "thunderstruck" by the passage of the Kansas-Nebraska Act. He saw at once that the bill took aim at America's moral heart—equality in law. Believing in this equality, the Founding Fathers had treated slavery as a necessary evil, to be confined to the original slave states. According to Lincoln, Douglas's bill assumed "that there can be moral right in the enslaving of one man by another."

From then on, Abraham concentrated largely on slavery. He did not hold political office, but he was a well-known Illinois politician, and he meant to challenge Douglas. The chance came in September, when Douglas returned to Illinois to defend his bill. Douglas was angry. He'd been burned in effigy and shouted down by outraged Northerners. He spoke all over the state. When Douglas reached the Springfield State Fair, Lincoln announced he would reply for antislavery extension voters and also give Douglas the chance to answer him. And at 2 p.m. on October 4, Lincoln gave his first great speech.

He began by saying, in his high, penetrating voice, that he was not there to abolish slavery. After all, it was allowed by the Constitution. But the Founding Fathers hid it away "as an afflicted man hides away a wen or a cancer, which he dares not cut out at once, lest he bleed to death."

He showed the steps the Founders had taken to keep slavery from spreading and he went on to describe the evil of the Kansas-Nebraska Act. Lincoln claimed the bill showed a "real zeal" for the spread of slavery and he said, "I hate it because of the monstrous injustice of slavery itself....because it...causes the real friends of freedom to doubt our sincerity...." For Lincoln, slavery degraded everyone, and he wanted to restrict it to the original slave states.

> *He showed the steps the Founders had taken to keep slavery from spreading and he went on to describe the evil of the Kansas-Nebraska Act.*

He also said Douglas was destroying American values. "Near eighty years ago we began by declaring that all men are created equal; but now from that beginning we have run down to the other declaration, that for some men to enslave others is a 'sacred right of self-government.'"

The act, he showed over and over again, promoted slavery over freedom, selfishness over justice, and defied the beliefs America was built on. He called for a return to the principles of the Declaration of Independence. Before his ringing finish,

Lincoln said the act would cause internal war.

His speeches were widely printed in pamphlets and newspapers, and antislavery politicians began to think that Lincoln had a chance at Illinois's second Senate seat.

For the Good of the Cause

With his popularity growing, Lincoln entered the race for Illinois's second Senate seat in 1855. In those days, Senators were chosen by state legislatures, and thanks to Stephen Douglas, the Illinois legislature was in turmoil. They all met at 3 p.m. on February 8, 1855, at the State Capitol. As the wintry day darkened, Mary Lincoln, along with other politicians' wives, sat in the gallery while the balloting went on and on.

At that point, Lincoln chose the antislavery cause over party loyalty and his own ambition.

It became clear that although Lincoln controlled a block of Whig votes, the tide was turning toward a pro-Douglas Democrat. At that point, Lincoln chose the antislavery cause over party loyalty and his own ambition. He told his aides to give his votes to the antislavery Democrat Lyman Trumbull. They did, and Trumbull won.

At a reception later, Lincoln cheerfully shook hands with Trumbull. Mary, however, couldn't forgive the man who took what she saw as her husband's rightful place. She also blamed Trumbull's wife, her own bridesmaid and the woman with whom she had written the letters in the *Sangamo Journal*, for not persuading Trumbull to give up his votes. Mary was capable of holding grudges, and even after a year had passed, when Julia Trumbull (formerly Julia Jayne) approached her one Sunday after church, " [Mary] turned her head the other way and pretended not to see me."

Antislavery Parties

The Free-Soilers organized in 1848 to try to stop slavery from reaching new territories. They came from both the Democrat Party and the Whigs and were briefly effective in the 1850s. Together with the Whigs, they helped create the Republican Party.

The American Party opposed slavery and non-Anglo-Saxon, non-Protestant immigrants from 1852 to 1856, when it dissolved. It arose from secret anti-immigration societies. Their members replied, "I know nothing," when questioned about their activities, so they were called "Know-Nothings."

The battle in the Illinois Capitol was going on all over the North. Southerners were proslavery. Northern Whigs and Democrats usually were not. But Northern Whigs were hopelessly split on how to deal with slavery. Some were extreme abolitionists and some belonged to various antislavery parties. The Whigs began to lose power, so in the spring of 1856, Lincoln helped shape the antislavery parties into the new Republican Party. It included abolitionists, former members of the Free-Soil Party, and former Whigs, and its goal was to oppose the "slave power."

The Whigs began to lose power, so in the spring of 1856, Lincoln helped shape the antislavery parties into the new Republican Party.

By 1856, the Union was in turmoil. Democrat James Buchanan had won the presidential election, but proceeded to divide the country even more. He pushed the Supreme Court toward its infamous Dred Scott decision (see page 63), which, he said, would settle the slavery debate. Instead, there was greater division because now there was a Federal ruling that said neither Federal nor territorial governments could prohibit slavery.

Even worse was the violence that was occurring in Kansas. Settlers entering the state were caught in a nightmare of burnings, beatings, riots, and murders by proslavery and antislavery factions fighting to gain power. Ultimately, Kansas was admitted to the Union as a free state, and the bloody struggle became known as "Bleeding Kansas."

The violence brought on by the Kansas-Nebraska Act is depicted in this 19th-century engraving, which shows pro-slavery Missourians traveling across state lines to burn the Free-Soil capital of Lawrence, Kansas.

The Lincoln-Douglas Debates

As each terrible event unfolded, Lincoln studied them with mounting fear for the country. Then, in June of 1857, Illinois Republicans nominated him as their "first and only choice" to run for the U.S. Senate against Stephen Douglas. Lincoln was a popular choice because he was the central organizer of their party,

Dred Scott Decision

Dred Scott was a Missouri slave whose owner took him to live first in free Louisiana Territory and then in free Illinois. Scott sued for release, based on his years in free territories.

When state courts ruled against him, he appealed to the U.S. Supreme Court. But Chief Justice Roger B. Taney wrote that black people were inferior beings with no rights to U.S. citizenship and no rights in the U.S. courts. He also declared that Congress could not forbid slavery in the territories. Abolitionists were horrified because slavery could now spread everywhere. The Dred Scott decision of 1857 helped bring America closer to civil war.

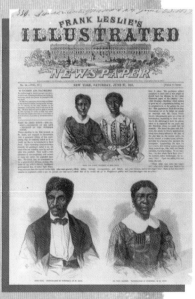

Following the Supreme Court ruling, an engraving of Dred Scott, his wife, and his two daughters was featured in a newspaper.

THE UNDECIDED POLITICAL PRIZE FIGHT.

As shown in this cartoon of the era, Stephen Douglas and Abraham Lincoln battled in the political ring on numerous occasions, including the race for the U.S. Senate in 1858 and for the presidency in 1860

author of eloquent antislavery speeches, and a principled man who had given up the chance for a Senate seat to help their cause.

Quoting the Bible at the Illinois Republican Convention, Lincoln said, "'A house divided against itself cannot stand.' I believe this government cannot endure, permanently half slave and half free. I do not expect the Union to be dissolved—I do not expect the house to fall—but I do expect it will cease to be divided." He rallied Republicans to unite against what he described as a conspiracy to make America a slave empire, and he promised "if we stand firm, we shall not fail."

Douglas paid close attention to Lincoln's speeches. "I shall have my hands full," he said. Lincoln "is as honest as he is shrewd, and if I beat him my victory will be hardly won."

Douglas was right. Challenged by Lincoln, he agreed to debate him in seven Illinois towns in the summer and fall of 1858. The men spoke to huge crowds. Each debate was like a giant fair, with floats, and signs, and songs, and shouting audiences.

Each debate was like a giant fair, with floats and signs and songs and shouting audiences.

Going into the debates, Douglas knew that although people might hate slavery, Illinois, like the rest of the country, was deeply racist. In speech after speech, he played on his audience's racial fears. He accused Lincoln of wanting to bring black people to Illinois, and of wanting blacks and whites to marry. At the debates, Douglas would shout, "If you desire Negro citizenship, if you desire to allow them to come into the state and settle with the white man, if you desire them to vote on an equality with yourselves....then support Mr. Lincoln and the black Republican party, who are in favor of the citizenship of the Negro." And each time the audiences would cry, "Never, never," and would cheer him loudly.

In his replies to Douglas's attacks, Lincoln explained that he believed in social and political equality for blacks. He said that he was not in favor of black people being voters or jurors, or

The Little Giant

Stephen Douglas, born in 1813, was a lawyer, judge, and the most powerful Democratic politician of his time in Illinois. He served as a U.S. congressman from 1843 to 1847 and as a senator from 1847 to 1861.

Even though Lincoln disagreed with Douglas on most political issues, Lincoln appreciated his opponent's successes. In a note to himself about Douglas, Lincoln wrote, "With *me* the race of ambition has been a failure, a flat failure. With *him* it has been one of splendid success. His name fills the nation and is not unknown, even in foreign lands."

Although small in stature, Stephen Douglas—nick-named the "Little Giant"—was one of Illinois' most influential politicians.

But Mary Lincoln was not as kind. Having once been courted by Douglas, she knew him better. "Mr. Douglas is a very little, little giant beside my tall Kentuckian, and intellectually my husband towers above Douglas just as he does physically." The fiery Douglas was only five feet four inches tall and was sometimes referred to as the "Little Giant."

husbands or wives of whites. But every time he said these things, he immediately returned to his basic premise: "We will not have peace in this country until the opponents of slavery arrest the further spread of it....In the right to eat the bread of his labor without the leave of anyone else, the slave is my equal and the equal of Judge Douglas, and the equal of every living man." He would continue and say to them that the Declaration of Independence made this equality before the law the primary principle of the nation. And Lincoln, too, was loudly cheered.

Lincoln said to his friends, "I feel like the boy who stumped his toe. I am too big to cry and too badly hurt to laugh."

Because of the wide reporting of these speeches and the great impression they made, historians say Lincoln won the debates. At the time, however, things were perceived differently, and the Illinois legislature, which was dominated by Democrats, reelected Douglas in 1858. Lincoln said to his friends, "I feel like the boy who stumped his toe. I am too big to cry and too badly hurt to laugh."

CHAPTER 8

A Run for the Presidency

Let us have faith that right makes might,
and in that faith, let us to the end, dare to do
our duty as we understand it.

After losing the Illinois senate race to Stephen Douglas, Lincoln was even more committed to blocking the spread of slavery to other states in the Union. Slavery was on everyone's mind, especially those of Southern slave owners, who feared they would be victims of violent slave revolts—such as the ones that had been led by John Brown, an avid abolitionist. A frenzy gripped the South. Armed militias were formed to help run Northerners out of town. And amid this explosive atmosphere was the upcoming presidential election of 1860.

Lincoln Is Nominated for President

With the Union strongly divided on the issue of slavery, the country approached another presidential election. It was 1860, and the Democratic Party was split. Northern Democrats nominated party leader Stephen Douglas, who ran on a popular sovereignty **plank**, but Southern Democrats wanted John C. Breckinridge, who was then the current vice president and favored an extremist platform that demanded a national slave code.

As for the Republicans, they passed over experienced party leaders and nominated Abraham

Raid on Harpers Ferry

John Brown, a Northern radical, was determined to abolish all slavery. He was not opposed to murdering slaveholders, and back in "Bleeding Kansas," along with six of his many sons, he had hacked five of them to avenge proslavery murders.

On the night of October 16, 1859, John Brown led eighteen men into Harpers Ferry, Virginia, where they attacked a U.S. armory. They had hoped to set up a base where they could aid runaway slaves and conduct attacks on slaveholders. But they were met, instead, with a day of murderous fighting. Colonel Robert E. Lee and a company of marines captured Brown and his men. They were quickly tried and hanged for treason and murder.

Brown went to his death as a martyr and said that he would forfeit his life and "mingle my blood with the....blood of millions in this slave country...." Southerners believed antislavery Republicans were behind the Harpers Ferry raid, especially when many Northerners called Brown a "crucified hero" and went into public mourning.

In this painting, c. 1884, artist Thomas Hovenden depicts abolitionist John Brown going to his death; a black child held by its mother gives Brown a farewell kiss.

Lincoln, a **dark horse** whose only national office was one term in Congress. Their choice was based on the divisions that had formed over the past few years. They knew antislavery Republicans could never win the South, which meant they had to win almost every free state in order to gain enough **electoral votes** for victory. The two other possible candidates were William H. Seward of New York, who was the Senate's most eloquent antislavery voice, and Salmon P. Chase of Ohio, who was a famed defender of runaway slaves. Both appeared too extreme.

The party leaders needed a moderate candidate. They looked back at the 1858 Lincoln-Douglas debates and remembered how Lincoln had spoken eloquently against the expansion of slavery. People everywhere wondered, "Who is this Lincoln we read about in the papers, who ran Douglas such a fine race?"

"Who is this Lincoln we read about in the papers, who ran Douglas such a fine race?"

Lincoln thought about the presidency that autumn as he traveled around the country, campaigning for Republicans. He was not openly running, not yet, but he was introducing himself to America and was positioning himself for a nomination.

As part of his campaign rhetoric, Douglas now claimed that the Founding Fathers had invented popular sovereignty by choosing not to rule on slavery questions. To Lincoln, this was dangerous nonsense because if Congress couldn't forbid slavery, slavery could be nationalized. And Lincoln wouldn't permit that to happen. If elected, the Republican Party would leave slavery alone where it existed in the South, but would block its spread into other states.

In some of his speeches, he made moving comparisons

The Electoral College

In a presidential election, the Constitution requires that each state appoint as many **electors** as the state has U.S. senators and representatives. In practice, each party in each state nominates a slate of electors. Following the popular vote of an election, the electors from each state cast their votes for the president and vice president. The candidate with the most electoral votes wins. Although electors from each state usually cast their votes for the candidate who has won the popular vote in their state, they are not bound by law to do so. And there have been times in history when they have not.

Because the number of electoral votes varies in each state, a candidate may lose the popular vote and win the election if he wins in enough states with large numbers of electors. Lincoln, for instance, lost ten Southern states in 1860 but won almost all the populous Northern states, to gain an electoral majority.

between the hopeless life of a slave and life in a free labor state. "I was a laborer," he pointed out, and explained that in a free society, everyone, including a lowly laborer, had hope for a better life.

Lincoln's speeches—peaceful, principled, and liberty loving—were printed and widely read. They convinced some of his old friends from the Eighth Circuit that Lincoln could be president. In January 1860, Judge David Davis, Norman Judd, Ward Hill Laymon, and Leonard Swett met secretly to launch a campaign for Lincoln.

Then, in February 1860, a speaking event catapulted

Lincoln into the public eye. Lincoln had been invited to address a grand audience of 1,500 at the Cooper Institute in New York City. He had spent three months researching the speech. Perhaps urged by Mary, he even bought a new suit.

On the day of the speech, a snowstorm raged outside, but the hall was packed. William Cullen Bryant, poet and editor, presented the tall, thin stranger as "an eminent citizen of the West, hitherto known only to you by reputation."

Stephen Douglas, Lincoln began, claimed that the Founding Fathers refused to legislate on slavery. But Lincoln countered and showed how twenty-one of the thirty-nine signers of the Constitution of 1787—a clear majority—had at one time or another voiced their opinion and advocated for the control and restriction of slavery to the original slave states. The Founding Fathers had not been silent on the matter. Douglas was wrong.

In 1860, the Cooper Institute, shown below, was the site where Lincoln delivered the speech that brought him national recognition.

He went on to address Southern accusations that Republicans incited John Brown. No one had implicated a single Republican for Harpers Ferry, Lincoln said. John Brown's action "was an attempt by white men to get up a revolt among slaves, in which the slaves refused to participate."

Lincoln also tried to present a fair point of view for the South. He said that if Southerners believed slavery was right, then "they are not to blame for desiring its full recognition, as being right; but, thinking it wrong, as we do, can we yield to them?" The answer, of course, was no.

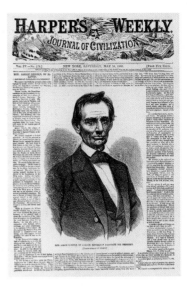

Harper's Weekly featured a story on Lincoln's triumph at Cooper Institute. The engraving of him was based on a photograph by Mathew Brady.

He ended his speech with a passionate call to duty: "LET US HAVE FAITH THAT RIGHT MAKES MIGHT, AND IN THAT FAITH, LET US TO THE END, DARE TO DO OUR DUTY AS WE UNDERSTAND IT."

He brought down the house. A man who was there said that when Lincoln spoke, his "face lighted up as with an inward fire; the whole man was transfigured....Presently I was on my feet with the rest, yelling like a wild Indian, cheering this wonderful man."

The speech would be reprinted thousands of times. Lincoln would go on to give it around New England. Now he was known by many more people.

By the time he returned home to Illinois in April, the local newspapers were endorsing the moderate Lincoln, a native son, for president. Lincoln admitted mildly, "The taste is in my mouth a little."

In early May, the Illinois State Republican Convention nominated him its candidate. It was there that Lincoln's cousin John Hanks appeared with some old fence rails, claiming that Abraham had split the rails himself as a boy. Thus, the symbol of the homespun prairie hero was born.

That year, the National Convention was held in Chicago. The Eighth Circuit crew, directed by Lincoln from Springfield, shrewdly pushed their message: Only Abraham Lincoln, a moderate, with no abolitionist ties, could carry the Lower North. After three **ballots**, Lincoln won the nomination to run as the Republican candidate for president of the United States.

When Lincoln, waiting in Springfield, got the message, he said, "There's a little woman down at our house would like to hear this. I'll go and tell her." As he walked the few blocks home, dancing crowds cheered him in the street.

Lincoln's Presidential Campaign

In those days, presidential candidates did not go out and campaign for themselves. Their supporters did it for them. Although bitterly disappointed at losing the nomination, Seward toured New England and the Midwest, giving speech after brilliant speech. Chase campaigned in Ohio. All over the North, there were huge rallies, parades, and floats featuring fence rails.

In each state, Republicans emphasized the parts of their overall platform that would get the most support. The first point was that there would be no extension of slavery. Naturalized citizens would be protected and would benefit from a homestead

In May 1860, the Republican National Convention, held in Chicago's "Wigwam," nominated Abraham Lincoln as their presidential candidate

act—an act offering free land in the West. This attracted land-hungry Irish and German immigrants, who were usually Democrats. A protective tariff would help industry and the working man's wages. And a railroad to the Pacific, as well as river and harbor improvements, would build business. Southern Democrats had opposed all of these issues for years.

During the campaign, mass hysteria swept the South. They feared that if the Republicans won the election, they would invade their states, free the slaves, and bring the South to ruin. In order to protect their way of life, they believed that the South must secede from the Union and form a new country, one where slavery would not be threatened.

Perhaps because Southerners had often threatened secession, Republicans didn't take them seriously. Lincoln himself said, "The people of the South have too much of good sense and

The Wide-Awake Club was a group of young Republican men who supported Lincoln in the presidential election. Their membership certificate shows a picture of Lincoln in the upper left and his running mate Hannibal Hamlin of Maine in the upper right.

good temper, to attempt the ruin of the government."

But Lincoln's democratic opponent Stephen Douglas recognized how serious the secession threat was. In October, after Republicans had won important state elections, Douglas knew he had lost his own chance for the presidency. To his credit, he said at once, "Mr. Lincoln is the next president. We must try to save the Union. I'll go South." And he did so bravely, arguing strongly against secession. But his words fell on deaf ears.

Lincoln Assumes the Presidency

Lincoln spent most of November 6, 1860—election day—in offices at the State House in Springfield. He sat in a tipped-back chair with his feet propped up on a woodstove, chatting with his friends "as calmly and amiably as if he had started on a picnic," a reporter said. At five he strolled home for supper. Later he was back in the State House, waiting for the returns.

They came in state by state. After midnight, he knew he'd won. He won every Northern state except New Jersey, where he split the vote with Douglas. Since Lincoln's name wasn't on the ballot in ten slave states, he won only 40 percent of the overall popular vote. But he had 180 electoral votes, well above the minimum 152. As church bells rang, he ran home, crying, "Mary, Mary, we are elected."

> *As church bells rang, he ran home, crying, "Mary, Mary, we are elected."*

Because inaugurations were held in March, Lincoln had four months to organize his government. There was bedlam as office-seekers swarmed into Springfield. A reporter from the *New York Tribune* admired Lincoln's tact with them and wrote that the **president-elect** was "the very embodiment of good temper and affability" with "a kind word, an encouraging smile, a humorous remark for nearly everyone.... [seeking] his presence...." At home, Mary sparkled as she gave nightly receptions for the visitors. Tad and Willie ran laughing among the crowds.

In these months, Lincoln chose his **cabinet**—the men who would advise him on all matters of the Union. Some presidents choose only men who will agree with them. Not Lincoln. He chose the strongest men from different regions, philosophies, and parties. Among them were some of his major rivals: William H. Seward, who became secretary of state, and Salmon P. Chase, who became secretary of the treasury. A

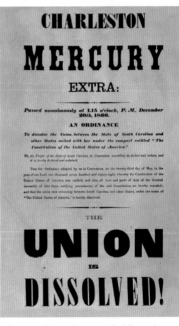

When South Carolina seceded from the Union in December 1860, the *Charleston Mercury* reported on this momentous event, which eventually led to the Civil War.

Some members of Lincoln's cabinet had been his rivals, but Lincoln still chose them because they were the best men for their particular positions.

minor rival, Edward Bates of Missouri, became attorney general. They were the best, he said.

While Lincoln worked, the deep South seceded, with South Carolina leading on December 20. Now a cloud hung over America. Seven states that had seceded banded together to form the Confederate States of America, with former Mississippi Senator Jefferson Davis as its president. Its cornerstone, said an official, was slavery.

Before Lincoln departed for Washington, he bid farewell to his elderly stepmother, Sally, and asked his old law partner, Billy Herndon, to leave their "Lincoln and Herndon" sign up. "If I live, I'm coming back some time, and then we'll go right on practicing law as if nothing had ever happened."

At last, on February 11, the president-elect left Springfield. Because of assassination rumors, he was accompanied by armed guards on the train. Mary, Willie, and Tad traveled separately. As

Lincoln paused on the windy railroad platform, he saw the thousands of people who had come to say good-bye. For a moment, tears filled his eyes. Then he said, "My friends—No one....can appreciate my feelings of sadness at this parting. To this place, and the kindness of these people, I owe everything. Here I have lived a quarter of a century, and passed from a young to an old man. Here my children have been born, and one is buried. I now leave, not knowing when, or whether ever, I may return, with a task before me greater than ever rested on Washington." He then blessed them and left.

President and Mrs. Lincoln lived in the White house with their two youngest sons, Willie (left) and Thomas (also called Tad, right). Their oldest son, Robert, was away at school during this time.

CHAPTER 9

An Untried President

We are not enemies but friends.
We must not be enemies.

Although crowds cheered Lincoln on his whistle-stop trip to Washington, he slipped into the city by night on secret trains because his colleagues felt certain that secessionists in Baltimore planned to assassinate him. When he arrived at his hotel room he found a threat-filled hate letter. Such letters made him "a little uncomfortable" at first, he later said, but he saved them all in an "Assassinations" file.

In the morning, Lincoln saw a Washington that was raw and unfinished. The Capitol bristled with scaffolding, awaiting a dome; the Washington Monument was only half-built; and the city smelled of the vast sewage marsh near the White House. Still, the spring trees were in bloom, and Washington was calm.

Lincoln's Inauguration

With secession and the formation of the Confederate States of America, America's conflict now centered on saving the Union, not on slavery. Lincoln said, "We must settle this question now, whether in a free government the minority have the right to break up the government whenever they choose. If we fail it will go far to prove the incapability of people to govern themselves." Still, the new

When Lincoln was inaugurated on March 4, 1861, the dome of the U.S. Capitol was still under construction.

president wanted to show the South that he would be fair, and he tried to do this with his inaugural address.

He delivered his speech on the bright, clear day of March 4 from the Capitol steps, with his family sitting behind him. President Buchanan, Chief Justice Taney, and Stephen Douglas, who supported the Union until he died a few months later, sat beside him. Douglas held Lincoln's hat when the president rose to speak.

He assured Southerners yet again that under the Constitution, he could not interfere with their slaves. But he made it clear that the federal government had authority over the whole country and it would hold its Southern properties. Unless attacked, the Union would not use force. Only the South could start a war.

He closed with words of hope: "We are not enemies but

friends. We must not be enemies. The mystic chords of memory, stretching from every battlefield and patriot grave, to every living heart and hearthstone, all over this broad land, will yet swell the chorus of the Union, when again touched....by the better angels of our nature."

At the Inaugural Ball that night, Mary was beautifully dressed in blue silk. She stayed at the ball for hours, but Lincoln went to bed early.

Chief Justice Roger Taney administered the presidential oath of office when Lincoln was first inaugurated.

Start of the Civil War

Even though he had tried to be firm but fair, the already inflamed South heard only threats in Lincoln's inaugural address. South Carolina responded at once. In March, Major Robert Anderson—whose sixty-man **garrison** defended U.S. Fort Sumter in Charleston Harbor—reported that he could not hold the fort against the scores of Confederate **batteries** now threatening him from shore. And he was running out of supplies.

The fort was a Union symbol, one that Lincoln had solemnly promised to "hold, occupy and possess." For weeks, the President and his Cabinet debated on what to do. Some wanted to surrender Sumter—but this would be a bow to Secessionists. Some

As the first lady, Mary Todd, seen in one of her many ball gowns, was the model of fashion in Washington society.

wanted to send in troop reinforcements—but this was warlike provocation. Finally, on April 6, Lincoln announced that he was sending provisions only—not troops—to Fort Sumter. They never arrived. On April 12, South Carolina troops fired at the fort, and Major Anderson surrendered.

The South had started a war. Amid wild excitement, Lincoln called for volunteers to crush the rebellion. When Lincoln did this, Virginia, Arkansas, North Carolina, and Tennessee joined the Confederacy. The border slave states of Missouri, Kentucky, and Maryland stayed in the Union. Eventually, Lincoln and his Cabinet would have a new army of a million volunteers and would organize a new navy to stop Southern shipping.

Both sides thought the war would be short. One Southern politician promised to use his handkerchief to wipe up all the blood that would be spilled. The North had great strengths: It

Following the Union's surrender of Fort Sumter, Confederate soldiers raised the Stars and Bars flag of the Southern Confederacy.

An 1863 map of the United States highlights the 11 Southern Confederate States: Alabama, Arkansas, Florida, Georgia, Louisiana, Mississippi, North Carolina, South Carolina, Tennessee, Texas, and Virginia.

had twice as many people as the South. It owned most of the railway system, most food farms, and almost all manufacturing, including weapons manufacturing.

To save the Union, the North had to bring down the Confederate government. That meant **blockading** the Confederate coast in order to stop imports. It also meant that Union armies had to invade unfamiliar Southern territory on many different fronts. For their part, Southerners had the advantage of home ground. But they also had many of the nation's best West Point–trained commanders join the Confederacy. Chief among them was Robert E. Lee.

Lee was the son of a grand Virginia family and was married to a daughter of Martha Washington. He was the best the army had to offer, and Lincoln offered him the Union command, but Lee turned him down and went to fight for the South instead.

Lee loathed the thought of civil war, but his loyalty was to Virginia. He said he could not raise his hand "against my relatives, my children, my home."

So the Union was left at first with Winfield Scott, a hero of the Mexican War and now frail and ill at seventy-five. His junior officers had not yet proved themselves. One of them, General Irwin McDowell, commanded the barely trained Army of the Potomac, stationed around Washington. In the weeks after Sumter, Union politicians and newspapers were demanding a battle to end the war quickly. McDowell's army was the one they wanted to move and press "on to Richmond," the Confederate capital.

McDowell knew his troops weren't ready. He told Lincoln his men were too green to win. "You are green, it is true," Lincoln

This 19th-century illustration depicts the first Battle of Bull Run, where Union soldiers under General Erwin McDowell were soundly defeated by Confederate troops.

said, "but they are green also; you are all green together." So in July 1861, federal troops marched twenty-five miles south of Washington and engaged a Southern army stationed at Manassas, Virginia. The battle, also known as the Battle of Bull Run, ended in a complete defeat for the North.

The President's Inner Circle

When news of the loss reached Washington, the city panicked. An army officer advised Mary Lincoln to take the children away for safety. "Will you go with us?" she asked Lincoln.

"Most assuredly I will not leave at this juncture."

"Then I will not leave you at this juncture," said Mary firmly, and she stepped with gusto into the role of first lady. Washington society thought her a crude Westerner, and she meant to prove them wrong. She started redecorating the White House, spending money wildly in the process. She also dressed herself as richly as an empress.

> " I will not leave at this juncture."

As a result the press criticized her extravagance, especially in wartime. When Lincoln discovered that she had overspent the congressional appropriation for the White House, he went into a rare fury. Soldiers didn't have blankets, he said, but his wife was buying "flubdubs for this damned old house." He said Mary would have to bear the blame, because he certainly wouldn't.

So Mary got some of her political friends to bury her mounting debts in other congressional **appropriations** and hide them in routine White House bills. But with all of her questionable behavior and her terrible temper, she was still the first lady, a loyal wife, a talented hostess, and a loving mother.

Her oldest boy, Robert, was away at Harvard University. But

the White House was home to her other two sons, Willie and Tad, who, like other young boys, kept crowds of pets, including ponies, goats, and kittens, and enjoyed building play forts.

Willie at ten was intelligent and gentle, "a counterpart of his father, save that he was handsome," Mary's cousin wrote. Eight-year-old Tad was temperamental, energetic, and friendly. He thought nothing of interrupting Cabinet meetings and would climb on Lincoln's knee and chatter away to everyone, even though a speech defect meant that few understood him.

His beloved boys helped keep Lincoln's spirits up during 1861. It was a grim year. Although Union troops made some progress in western Virginia, there were no great victories and many defeats—not only at Manassas but also in Missouri, Kentucky, and Virginia. The newspapers blamed the president, but the people who worked closely with him knew better and appreciated his great qualities.

His beloved boys helped keep Lincoln's spirits up during 1861. It was a grim year.

One cabinet member in particular, Secretary of State William Seward, admired the president immensely. But Seward had begun his job with some bitterness because he felt Lincoln had stolen his own chances for the presidency. When he was asked to join Lincoln's cabinet, he expected to run the government, with "the little Illinois lawyer" as a figurehead. But Lincoln took firm control immediately and was so tactful that soon Seward wrote that Lincoln's spirit "was almost superhuman." He added, "The President is the best of us."

The two became friends and visited often. Because Seward was a short man, he and the tall president made an odd-looking pair when they were seen together. They were both devoted to work, conversation, and wisecracks. Seward often recounted how he once found Lincoln polishing his shoes and remarked that in Washington, "we do not blacken our own boots." "Indeed." replied Lincoln, "Then whose boots do you blacken, Mr. Secretary?"

Lincoln's generous spirit—and shrewdness—lay behind a choice he made early in 1862. His War Department was a mess. Dishonest dealers had sold the Union army guns that wouldn't fire, clothes that fell apart, and sick horses. The war secretary had to go. In his place, Lincoln chose the exceptionally bright and hard-driving Edwin Stanton—the man who had treated him so cruelly during the McCormick vs. Manny case in Cincinnati five years before. Lincoln never wasted time with grudges, and Stanton took on the job and swiftly reformed the War Department.

He also came to admire the president. Stanton's secretary observed that no two men could have been less alike. "Lincoln was as calm and unruffled as the summer sea in moments of

Thomas (Tad) Lincoln loved to play with animals. This photograph (taken between 1860 and 1865) shows him sitting on his pony.

greatest peril; Stanton would lash himself into a fury....yet no two men ever did or could work better in harness."

In February 1862, both of the Lincoln boys came down with typhoid from Washington's filthy water. It was fatal to Willie, who suffered for weeks, only to die on February 20. His mother and father mourned differently. Mary collapsed completely. Lincoln burst into his secretary's office sobbing "my boy is gone—he is actually gone," but in the months afterward, as Mary hid in her room, Lincoln buried himself in work. He kept little Tad close to him so that the boy would not be lonely.

William Seward was Lincoln's secretary of state. This 1865 lithograph shows the two together as President Lincoln signed the Emancipation Proclamation.

The Dark War Years

The death of Willie was the sad beginning to a dark year for both Lincoln and the Union. At first, the Union seemed to be advancing, especially in the West. In April, Northern general Ulysses S. Grant defeated a Southern army at the bloody Battle of Shiloh, in Tennessee. It was all-out war, and the death toll on both sides was rising into the tens of thousands.

In Washington, General George McClellan took command of the Army of the Potomac and trained it brilliantly, but he was

ultimately a poor leader in battle. Robert E. Lee took command
of the Confederate army and the tide began to turn. In a series
of savage June battles known as the "Seven Days," Lee shattered
McClellan's army and pushed it back to the James River.

A Plan for Emancipation

Meanwhile, Congress and the cabinet argued over slavery.
Liberal Republicans pressed the president to free the slaves.
Conservatives objected, citing what the Constitution says
concerning slavery, in particular, the notorious three-fifths
clause and also the law concerning runaway slaves. As for the
general public, few had sympathy for the black slaves.

Lincoln needed a way to present the idea of emancipation—
the freeing of slaves—in terms the public would accept. He
explained that Confederate soldiers were free to fight because
their slaves built their forts, dug their trenches, and farmed
their fields. He reasoned that freed slaves could help the
Union army win the war. In essence, emancipation was a
military necessity and the president's war powers could
override the Constitution.

In the summer of 1862, Lincoln told his
cabinet that emancipation was "absolutely essential
for the salvation of the Union." The proposal he
suggested promised that all slaves living in a
territory that was still in rebellion on January 1,
1863, would be freed. Seward wisely pointed out
that a summer of defeats was a bad time to issue the

Photographed a year before his death in
1862, William, the third son of the Lincolns,
died of typhoid at the age of 11.

Following a Northern victory at Antietam, President Lincoln visits General George McClellan at the Union headquarters.

proposal because "it may be viewed as the last measure of an exhausted government." He suggested waiting for a Northern victory.

The victory was weeks in coming. In early autumn, General Lee invaded Maryland, which was Union territory. George McClellan's army drove him back to Virginia on September 17, at the Battle of Antietam. With 24,000 men lost to both sides, Antietam was the bloodiest one-day battle of the Civil War.

Still, Northern morale skyrocketed. Antietam gave Lincoln his victory. On September 22, he issued the Preliminary Emancipation Proclamation. Many abolitionists celebrated. "We shout for joy that we live to record this righteous decree," wrote abolitionist Frederick Douglass, who was himself a former slave. The final proclamation would soon come. Douglass trusted that Lincoln would keep his word and said, "If he has taught us to confide in nothing else, he has taught us to confide in his word."

Frederick Douglass

A great abolitionist and superb orator, Frederic Douglass was born a Maryland slave in 1817 or 1818. His owner's wife taught him to read, and he taught himself to write.

In 1838 he escaped to New York, and after a few weeks, moved to New Bedford, Massachusetts, where he began to speak out against slavery. He was so eloquent that abolitionists eventually bought his freedom. In 1845, his autobiography was published, and three years later he established an influential antislavery newspaper called the *North Star*.

During the Civil War, Douglass served as an adviser to President Lincoln and fought for the rights of black regiments. At first a critic of Lincoln, Douglass came to be a staunch admirer of the president.

Frederick Douglass (in a photograph taken between 1865 and 1880) was born a slave, but escaped to freedom and became one of the most influential abolitionists of his time.

CHAPTER 10

Trial by Fire

With malice toward none, with charity for all…let us strive on…to bind up the nation's wounds….

Early on New Year's Day, 1863, Abraham Lincoln edited his final Emancipation Proclamation. It declared that all slaves in rebellious states not already under Union control were now free and could join the Union army. While it did not free slaves in border states like Maryland and Kentucky, it was a first step. He sent it to the State Department to be copied. It would be hours before he signed it to make it official.

In the meantime, the president attended his annual New Year's open house—when any citizen could come in and meet him. The White House doors were thrown open and thousands of people poured in to shake Lincoln's hands.

At last Lincoln met with Secretary of State Seward, who'd brought the final Proclamation. The president took up his pen and then paused. His hand trembled from

This commemorative lithograph, c. 1888, carried the text of the Emancipation Proclamation along with a portrait of Lincoln.

hours of handshakes. If the signature wobbled, Lincoln remarked, people would say, "He hesitated." So he rested. Then he carefully wrote his name.

Coolly, Lincoln awaited reactions. Republican newspapers supported him, but racist Democratic editorials called the proclamation "a wicked…and revolting deed." They claimed that white soldiers wouldn't serve with blacks. The War Department started recruiting anyway. Within a year, 180,000 black soldiers were fighting for the Union, even though they received less pay than their white counterparts and were segregated as a group.

But the army needed even more men to fight in the war. In March, Lincoln issued a **draft law**. The North exploded into antidraft and anti-black riots. Democrats organized a peace movement, demanding compromise with the South. But Lincoln refused to compromise with the South or back down on his Emancipation Proclamation. "You say you will not fight to free negroes," he would write in a public letter, adding, "some of them seem willing to fight for you."

The Battle Rages On

To raise Northern spirits, Lincoln needed a battle victory, but in 1863, that was difficult. Union armies stalled in Tennessee and Mississippi. In Virginia, things were worse. The year before, Lincoln had replaced George McClellan as Commander of the Army of the Potomac with Ambrose Burnside, who promptly lost the Battle of Fredericksburg and 13,000 men. Lincoln then replaced Burnside with Joseph "Fighting Joe" Hooker, a West Pointer who'd done well at Antietam and Fredericksburg.

Hooker was a loudmouth and a hothead, and Lincoln wanted to see how this confident commander was handling his

Black Union Soldiers

The 1863 Emancipation Proclamation gave blacks the right they had long asked for—to fight in the Union army. Although black soldiers were supposed to be limited to guard and labor duty, many formed fighting regiments and impressed white troops with their bravery in battle.

The most famed black regiment was the 54th Massachusetts. In July 1863, during the Union campaign against Charleston, the 54th led the charge on Fort Wagner, near the harbor. The regiment lost half its men and had to fall back, but its heroism became a legend.

Such performances helped Frederick Douglass win his fight for equal pay for black soldiers. As Douglass said, "Once let the black man get upon his person the brass letters, U.S.; let him get an eagle on his button, and a musket on his shoulder…and there is no power…which can deny that he has earned the right of citizenship in the United States."

This 1863 lithograph depicts the battle of Fort Wagner, where black soldiers of the 54th Massachusetts Regiment bravely led the charge, only to lose half of their men.

Following one of the Chancellorsville campaigns in 1863, photographer Mathew Brady captured this picture of Union soldiers burying their dead.

charge. So in April, he took Mary and Tad down the coast from Washington to join the Union camp at Falmouth, Virginia. There was a grand cavalry review with soldiers on horse-back riding by and sunlight glittering on ranks of bayonets. Lincoln rode along the lines, greeting the troops. Young Tad followed on a pony, his legs sticking out on either side, steadied by a general's orderly—a thirteen-year-old bugler who'd been in the army for two years.

It was a magnificent sight, but Lincoln also spent hours with the wounded. He knew the price of war, and Hooker's boasting about the victories he was going to win annoyed the president. He warned the general, "The hen is the wisest of all animal creation, because she never cackles until the egg is laid."

He was right to be worried. In May, Hooker, with more than

130,000 Union soldiers, faced Robert E. Lee, who had less than half that number of rebel troops at Chancellorsville, Virginia. In a brilliant effort—still known as "Lee's Perfect Battle"—Lee split his smaller army and attacked the confused Hooker on two fronts, sending the Army of the Potomac into retreat. The defeat cost the Union 17,000 men.

Made bold by his victory at Chancellorsville, Lee marched toward Pennsylvania. It was another invasion. Hooker panicked. He said (wrongly) that the rebels outnumbered him. Lincoln replaced him with George Meade, who began moving the army into Pennsylvania to intercept Lee. In July 1863, the armies met at the town of Gettysburg.

Made bold by his victory at Chancellorsville, Lee marched toward Pennsylvania. It was another invasion.

Although Lincoln had moved to a garden community three miles from the city to escape the Washington heat, he stayed at the telegraph room in the War Department and slept on a couch so he could see the war dispatches as soon as they came in. The fighting at Gettysburg went on for three days, killing or wounding 40,000 men. This was Lee's attempt to crush the Union army, attacking from both sides and staging a fierce, doomed charge of 15,000 men against entrenched Union troops.

Then, on July 3, word came that Lee was in retreat. The Army of the Potomac, after so many losses, had won a spectacular victory and had dealt the South a critical blow. Lee had lost nearly a third of his army.

The next day, July 4, the usually dignified Navy Secretary Gideon Welles entered Lincoln's office and threw his hat in the air. Ulysses S. Grant had taken Vicksburg, Mississippi, after a

Dead soldiers are shown sprawled across the battlefield of Gettysburg, Pennsylvania. Casualties from this battle—both Union and Confederate—numbered in the tens of thousands.

siege of forty-six days. Now the Union controlled the entire Mississippi Valley—the western South—and the Mississippi River, the crucial waterway of the Confederacy. As Lincoln said, "The Father of Waters again goes unvexed to the sea."

With victory came hope. All through that steaming summer, while Mary and Tad vacationed in New England, Lincoln continued to work calmly. One of his secretaries wrote to the other, using their private nickname for the president, "The Tycoon is in fine whack. I have rarely seen him more serene & busy. He is managing this war, the draft, foreign relations, and planning a reconstruction of the Union, all at

"There is no man in the country, so wise so gentle and so firm."

once....There is no man in the country, so wise so gentle and so firm."

Lincoln handled his endless work well partly because he knew how to relax. He'd go to the Navy Yard to see great guns being tested. He'd test new rifles himself behind the White House. Most of all, Lincoln loved the theater. One of his assistants noticed how intently he followed a performance of Shakespeare's *Henry IV, Part One* and commented, "He has forgotten the war. He has forgotten Congress. He is out of politics. He is living in Prince Hal's time."

Honoring the Dead

For Lincoln, the central question of the war was whether the promise of equal rights and self government stated in the Declaration of Independence could be kept. On November 19, 1863, he put that question into words that would echo through the ages.

A new National Soldiers' Cemetery was to be dedicated at the battlefield of Gettysburg, where only a few months before, thousands of soldiers, both Union and Confederate, had died in one of the bloodiest battles of the war. The main speaker scheduled was the orator Edward Everett, former governor of Massachusetts, who spoke for two hours. Then, as bright sunshine lighted the bloodied battlefield, still strewn with horse skeletons and coffins, Lincoln stood up and read his dedication in his high, penetrating voice. He spoke briefly but so movingly about Union goals and sacrifices that the 9,000 people listening were stunned into silence for a moment before they began to applaud.

Edward Everett wrote that the president had caught the meaning of the battle better in two minutes than he had in two hours. As Secretary Seward said, "No one but Abraham Lincoln could have made that speech." The president—"Father Abraham" to the Union troops—was the symbol of dedication and determination.

The Embattled President and Generals

In March 1864, Lincoln made Grant General in Chief of all the Union armies. A shy and plain-spoken man, Grant never complained, never asked for more troops, and worked with determination to get the job done. "I can't spare this man," Lincoln said. "He fights." Together they worked out a plan to

An undated print depicts President Lincoln giving his dedication address on the battlefield of Gettysburg on November 19, 1863.

The Gettysburg Address

Fourscore and seven years ago our fathers brought forth on this continent a new nation, conceived in liberty and dedicated to the proposition that all men are created equal. Now we are engaged in a great civil war, testing whether that nation or any nation so conceived and so dedicated can long endure. We are met on a great battlefield of that war. We have come to dedicate a portion of that field as a final resting place for those who here gave their lives that that nation might live. It is altogether fitting and proper that we should do this.

But in a larger sense, we cannot dedicate, we cannot consecrate, we cannot hallow this ground. The brave men, living and dead who struggled here have consecrated it far above our poor power to add or detract. The world will little note nor long remember what we say here, but it can never forget what they did here.

It is for us the living rather to be dedicated here to the unfinished work which they who fought here have thus far so nobly advanced. It is rather for us to be here dedicated to the great task remaining before us—that from these honored dead we take increased devotion to that cause for which they gave the last full measure of devotion—that we here highly resolve that these dead shall not have died in vain, that this nation under God shall have a new birth of freedom, and that government of the people, by the people, for the people shall not perish from the earth.

destroy the Confederacy and wipe out its armies by slashing in from all sides—Georgia, Alabama, and Virginia, which is where Grant stationed himself.

It was a long, hard summer. In Georgia, the Southerners dug in hard around Atlanta, protecting that important city from William Tecumseh Sherman's determined assault. In Virginia, Grant's repeated attacks on Lee's army around the town of Spotsylvania Courthouse repeatedly failed. Grant's casualties in this campaign rose to 50,000. The newspapers began to despair about the death toll. But Grant was a stubborn man. "I propose to fight it out on this line if it takes all summer," he said.

Grant believed that only total destruction of the Confederacy would end the war. Confederate troops under General Jubal Early swept through the Shenandoah Valley to the edge of Washington. Grant ordered Philip Sheridan to drive Early out and lay waste to the fertile Shenandoah. No food from there would feed the rebels.

Lincoln was as embattled as his general in 1864. It was a presidential election year, and he wanted badly to be reelected. It would show that the people believed in his war policies. He had plenty of critics in the war-weary Union. The loudest were Democrats. They hated the war, the Emancipation Proclamation, and Abraham Lincoln. They put together a party platform

A lithograph, c. 1868, shows a full portrait of General Ulysses S. Grant, Chief of all the Union Armies. A West Point graduate, Grant had previously fought in the Mexican War.

In 1864, General Sherman captured and occupied the city of Atlanta. He and his staff are shown here at Federal Fort No. 7 in Atlanta.

that demanded peace at any price. But even their presidential nominee—none other than Lincoln's former general, George McClellan—wouldn't support it. He said he would fight on until the Union was restored. But he wouldn't fight for emancipation.

Lincoln's own party criticized him—conservatives because he moved too quickly on emancipation, radicals because he moved too slowly. Still, they nominated Lincoln. Their platform included the president's deepest desire—a proposed Thirteenth Amendment to the Constitution outlawing slavery forever.

The war limped along. By August, Lincoln was privately convinced that despairing voters would elect McClellan. Mary was frightened at the idea. She'd had a bad four years, and she still mourned Willie. To ease her grief, Mary visited spiritualists who claimed they could reach him. She believed Willie's spirit visited her every night, "with the same, sweet adorable smile he always had...."

At this time, Mary received almost as much newspaper abuse as the president. Her Kentucky brothers were fighting and dying for the Confederacy, and she received letters calling her a rebel spy. "Why should I sympathize with the rebels?" she asked. "They would hang my husband tomorrow if it was in their power...."

On top of everything else, Mary's crazy spending trips (she bought 300 pairs of gloves at one time) had left her $27,000 in debt. If Lincoln lost, the bills would go to him. She begged politicians to help her out—without telling Lincoln, who she said, was "almost a monomaniac on the subject of honesty."

Then, in early fall, the Republicans got a boost. On September 3, Union General William Tecumseh Sherman wired Washington, "Atlanta is ours, and fairly won." The queen city of the Deep South had fallen. Its citizens were driven out into the countryside, and much of Atlanta was

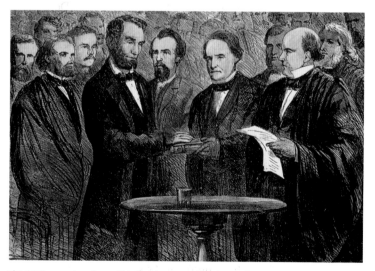

This 1865 engraving shows Chief Justice Samuel P. Chase administering the oath of office to President Lincoln during the president's second inauguration.

burned to the ground. "We are going to be wiped off the face of the earth," wrote a Southern diarist.

Then, in October, Philip Sheridan pounded rebel troops in the Shenandoah Valley. After he drove them out, he destroyed the valley's crops and livestock. The Confederacy was dying, and with it the Democrats' hopes. In November, Lincoln won the presidency by just over 400,000 popular votes (and almost all the soldiers' votes). He had 212 electoral votes to McClellan's 21.

That winter brought triumphs to the Union and horror to the Confederacy. General Sherman marched his huge army from Atlanta to the sea, taking or destroying nearly everything in his path. "We cannot change the hearts of those people.... but we can make war so terrible....that generations would pass away before they would again appeal to it," he said. In December he took Savannah, Georgia.

The Confederacy was dying, and with it the Democrats' hopes.

As the South trembled, Lincoln reached out a hand of peace in his second inaugural address. He said that perhaps God had visited the terrible war on both North and South as a punishment for tolerating slavery. But both sides now might come together, cleansed, he said, and he ended with these famous words: "With malice toward none, with charity for all....let us strive on....to bind up the nation's wounds; to care for him who shall have borne the battle, and for his widow, and his orphan—to do all which may achieve and cherish a just, and a lasting peace, among ourselves, and with all nations."

During his address, the president saw Frederick Douglass, who was a very tall man, standing in the crowd. He didn't see, standing behind him, a famous actor named John Wilkes Booth.

CHAPTER 11

The End of a Great Era

Now he belongs to the ages.

—*Secretary Edwin Stanton*

Preoccupied and exhausted by the war, Lincoln saw little of his wife. He never discussed war matters with her, for he knew she was somewhat indiscreet. For her part, Mary anxiously hid her debts from him and complained of neglect.

However, by the spring of 1865, spirits began to rise. Lincoln's reelection proved that his countrymen stood behind him. With his urging, Congress passed the Thirteenth Amendment to the Constitution, which guaranteed that slaves would be forever free. Lincoln had wanted this amendment because he knew that his Emancipation Proclamation needed to be supplemented by a permanent change to the Constitution.

A congressional resolution signed by President Lincoln approved the 13th Amendment, which ended the practice of slavery forever. The amendment was ratified on December 6, 1865.

The Civil War Ends

By this time, the Civil War was drawing to a close. A starving and devastated South hung on grimly, but most of it was under Union control, and Union armies were closing in on General Robert E. Lee's Army of Virginia.

In March, Lincoln and Mary saw the battlefront, when they visited General Ulysses S. Grant at his Virginia headquarters. With their son Robert, who was serving as an aide to Grant, they toured the battlefields and hospitals. Then on April 3, Richmond, capital and heart of the Confederacy, fell and was burned to the ground by fleeing rebel troops. When the Confederate

When the Confederate government fled, Lincoln walked the city streets, surrounded by freed slaves, singing for joy.

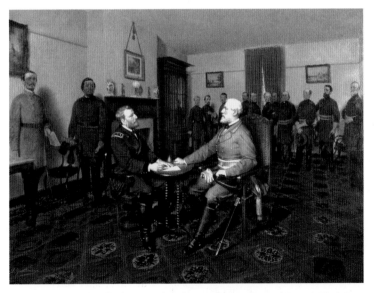

This 1867 painting depicts the surrender of General Lee to General Grant in Virginia on April 9, 1865.

government fled, Lincoln walked the city streets, surrounded by freed slaves who were singing for joy.

At last, on April 9, totally surrounded, General Lee surrendered his once-unbeatable army to General Ulysses S. Grant at Appomattox Courthouse, in Virginia. Grant would write that he felt only sadness "at the downfall of a foe who had fought so long and valiantly and had suffered so much for a cause....one of the worst for which a people ever fought." He ordered his troops not to fire victory salutes because, "the rebels are our countrymen again."

When news of the surrender arrived, War Secretary Edwin Stanton ordered a 500-gun artillery salute. Bands marched through the streets of Washington, which were wreathed in its spring blossoms. At night, the windows in every government building, including the Capitol, with its new dome, blazed with candle- and lamplight.

On the morning of Friday, April 14, Lincoln attended his regular cabinet meeting. Then he and Mrs. Lincoln went for a carriage ride in the afternoon. Mary commented that she was startled by his cheerfulness. He replied that he might well feel cheerful, with the war's end. Then he added, "We must *both*,

A victorious but tired President Lincoln was photographed on April 10, 1865, just four days before his death.

be more cheerful in the future—between the war & the loss of our darling Willie—we have both, been very miserable."

Lincoln's Assassination

That night the Lincolns planned to go to Ford's Theatre on Tenth Street to see *Our American Cousin*, a British farce. They took along Major Henry Rathbone and his fiancée, Clara Harris, the daughter of a friend of Mary's.

About a block away from the theater, John Wilkes Booth met with three conspirators. Booth was the brother of the noted Shakespearean actor (and Lincoln favorite) Edwin Booth and was an actor himself. Unlike his brother, John was pro-South and violently anti-black. He blamed the Confederacy's defeat on Lincoln. Once he had thought to kidnap the president, but now he decided to kill Lincoln—as well as William Seward and Vice President Johnson.

Booth's little team, as historian Bruce Catton remarked,

Assassin John Wilkes Booth used this small derringer to shoot and kill President Lincoln at Ford's Theatre.

consisted of a "set of dimwitted incompetents who could hardly have carried out a plan to rob a corner newsstand." Lewis Payne, an ex–Confederate soldier, and David Herold, a drugstore clerk, were to kill William Seward at the secretary's home. George Atzerodt, a carriage maker, was to murder Vice President Johnson at his hotel. Booth would take the president.

Payne, pretending to deliver medicine to Seward— who had been previously injured in a carriage accident— entered Seward's house. Then, in a frenzy, he pistol-whipped several people there, including two of Seward's sons, a State Department messenger, and Seward himself, before running off into the night. Blood was everywhere, but all survived. The attempt on Johnson's life never occurred because Atzerodt decided he was a kidnapper, not a murderer, and ran away.

Outside the box, Lincoln's guard, a lazy drunk who had gotten the job because of a bureaucratic mix-up, wandered away from his post.

Booth was more successful. He had performed in plays at Ford's Theatre before and actually received his mail there, so people were accustomed to seeing him around. When the president's party arrived, Booth was already in the theater. He watched Lincoln step into his flag-draped box and heard the orchestra playing "Hail to the Chief" as the audience gave the president a rousing standing ovation. Outside the box, Lincoln's guard, a lazy drunk who had gotten the job because of a bureaucratic mix-up, wandered away from his post.

At 10:12 p.m., Booth gave his calling card to the footman who manned the anteroom of the presidential box. The footman let the eminent actor in. Booth peered through a spy hole in the door of the box to locate the president, who was sitting in a rocking chair. Then Booth opened the door and fired a pistol directly into the back of Abraham Lincoln's head.

As Lincoln slumped forward, the women screamed. Major Rathbone immediately tackled Booth, who pulled a knife and stabbed the major in the chest. Booth quickly leaped from the box onto the stage below, catching his spur on a draped flag and breaking his leg. He

> *"They have shot the President!"*

raised his dagger and shouted the Virginia state motto, *Sic semper tyrannus*, meaning "Thus always to tyrants." He then vanished into the side wings of the stage.

This 1865 lithograph by Currier & Ives depicts John Wilkes Booth shooting President Lincoln at Ford's Theatre. Mrs. Lincoln and friends of the president sat alongside him in the presidential box.

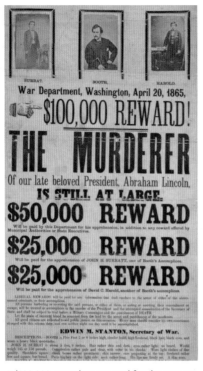

War Department, Washington, April 20, 1865,

$100,000 REWARD!

THE MURDERER

Of our late beloved President, Abraham Lincoln,

IS STILL AT LARGE.

$50,000 REWARD

Will be paid by this Department for his apprehension, in addition to any reward offered by Municipal Authorities or State Executives.

$25,000 REWARD

Will be paid for the apprehension of JOHN H. SURRATT, one of Booth's Accomplices.

$25,000 REWARD

Will be paid for the apprehension of David C. Harold, another of Booth's accomplices.

EDWIN M. STANTON, Secretary of War.

A $100,000 reward was posted for the capture of Lincoln's assassin and others involved in the crime.

"They have shot the President!" Mary screamed. A nearby doctor rushed in and found the bullet hole at the base of the president's skull. It had lodged in his brain, behind his right eye. "His wound is mortal," said the doctor. "It is impossible for him to recover." But he gave the president artificial respiration until he breathed on his own, and then had him carried to the Peterson House, a boarding house that was across the street. They laid him aslant on a bed, for it was too short for his long frame.

Word went out immediately. From all over Washington, Lincoln's cabinet members and friends rushed to the house. Robert came from the White House, saw his father's terrible injury, and broke down. He tried to comfort his mother, who was sobbing in the parlor, but she hardly recognized him. Outside, a silent crowd gathered.

All through that long night, Lincoln's friends kept vigil. War Secretary Stanton, his voice thick with tears, took charge. He suspended civilian government and put Washington under

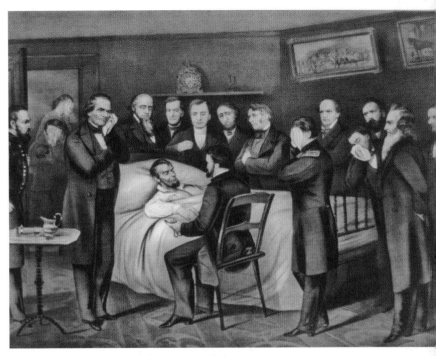

An 1865 lithograph shows Lincoln on his deathbed surrounded by his family and friends. When Lincoln died on April 15, 1865, Vice President Andrew Johnson assumed the presidency.

military control; he then arranged guards for Vice President Andrew Johnson, who would soon become the new president. Stanton found a judge to help him take down testimony from witnesses and then organized a search throughout the city and countryside to bring in the suspects.

As a dark, rainy dawn approached, the death struggle began, and everyone gathered at Lincoln's bedside. Most of them wept. At 7:22 a.m., on April 15, 1865, Abraham Lincoln died. Secretary Stanton, standing by the bed, said, "Now he belongs to the ages."

The conspirators of Lincoln's assassination were captured and tried. On July 7, 1865, they were hanged at the Washington, D.C., arsenal.

As for Booth, he died ten days later in a shootout with soldiers in a burning tobacco barn. The rest of the conspirators— and others who had helped them—were tried by a military court. Two were imprisoned and the rest were hanged.

The funeral service for the first American president ever to be assassinated was held in the East Room of the White House, but it would be two weeks before he was laid to rest in his beloved Illinois. Millions mourned "Father Abraham." He had led them through a great national trial to safety. They had listened to him, voted for him, and flocked to his armies. Now they gathered to bid farewell as he lay in state at the Capitol in Washington.

Then, day and night, silent crowds lined the railroad tracks as his great funeral train, draped in black, steamed westward. It made numerous stops along the way, where various ceremonies

President Lincoln's funeral procession is shown moving down Pennsylvania Avenue to the Capitol, where he lay in state for two days before making the long journey back to Illinois for burial.

were held for the great president. Reaching his final destination, Lincoln was buried at last in Springfield, with his dead sons, Willie and Eddie, beside him.

During this entire time, Mary Lincoln was conspicuously absent. After Lincoln had died, Robert took her to the White House, where she collapsed. For a month, the house echoed with "the wails of a broken heart, the unearthly shrieks, the terrible convulsions." She finally left on May 23, the day of the Union army's victory march through the city. No one came to say good-bye.

Her final years were desperately sad, for in her grief, Mary grew eccentric. She moved to Europe, drifting from city to spa town, keeping Tad with her. She cherished his "tender treatment of me at all times." When they finally returned home, Tad contracted a lung infection, and at the age of eighteen, he died in July 1871.

With her husband and three of her sons dead, Mary clung to and quarreled with Robert, now a lawyer, and his new wife. She insisted on living in hotels. Her shopping binges and her belief that she saw spirits convinced Robert that she was going mad, and in 1875, he had her committed to an asylum—a betrayal she never forgave. She left the hospital to spend her last years as a recluse, hiding in the

Of Lincoln's four sons, only Robert, the eldest, survived his father. He eventually served as secretary of war under President James Garfield.

Springfield house of her sister Elizabeth, where she'd met Abraham all those years before. She died in 1882 and joined Abraham, Eddie, Willie, and Tad in the Springfield tomb.

Robert went his own successful way. He served as secretary of war, Minister to Great Britain, and finally became a railroad **magnate**. When he died in 1926, he was buried in Arlington National Cemetery, not with the other Lincolns. His wife said he wanted to be his own man.

Lincoln's Legacy

Following the death of this great president, the Union that Lincoln had preserved went through a difficult period of reconstruction. The slaves that he had set free were not met with open arms, but with severe acts of discrimination, intimidation, and lynching.

Not until the civil rights movement of the 1950s and '60s would African Americans begin to enjoy their basic rights.

Nevertheless, Lincoln had set African Americans free, and in doing so, was able to steadfastly hold to the

Not until the Civil Rights Movement of the 1950s and '60s would African Americans begin to enjoy their basic rights.

principles of American democracy—that all men are created equal under the law. In leading the nation through this great Civil War, he had forged its separate regions into one nation.

Harriet Beecher Stowe, the renowned author of *Uncle Tom's Cabin*, believed that no other man could have saved the Union. She wrote, "Surrounded by all sorts of conflicting claims, by traitors, by half-hearted, timid men, by Border States men, and Free States men, by radical Abolitionists and Conservatives, he has listened to all, weighed the words of all, waited, observed, yielded now here and now there, but in the main kept one inflexible, honest purpose, and drawn the national ship through."

IN THIS TEMPLE
AS IN THE HEARTS OF THE PEOPLE
FOR WHOM HE SAVED THE UNION
THE MEMORY OF ABRAHAM LINCOLN
IS ENSHRINED FOREVER

The Lincoln Memorial in Washington, D.C., was dedicated on Memorial Day 1922. Inscribed on the walls of the monument are Lincoln's Gettysburg Address and his second inaugural address.

Uncle Tom's Cabin

Harriet Beecher Stowe's *Uncle Tom's Cabin* was inspired by the Fugitive Slave Law passed by Congress in 1850—a law that outraged the North. It permitted slave catchers to cross state lines to capture escapees, and it gave those escapees no rights to **habeas corpus**—the Constitutional right to appear before a judge to determine whether one's arrest is legal.

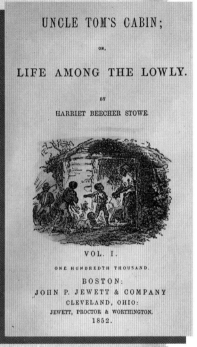

Horrified, Mrs. Stowe, wife of a Congregationalist minister and mother of six, sat down to write her influential book. The novel's vivid and heartbreaking images of slave life and its story of escape riveted readers, both North and South. Published in 1852, it sold 300,000 copies in the United States the first year.

Harriet Beecher Stowe's *Uncle Tom's Cabin* brought the evils of slavery to light. The title page of her 1852 first edition is shown.

No one said the book was great literature, but no one denied its power. When President Lincoln met Mrs. Stowe in 1862, he supposedly remarked to her, "So you're the little woman who wrote the book that made this great war."

Glossary

abolitionists—those in favor of ending slavery.

apportionment—the distribution of representative seats within the U.S. House of Representatives, which is based on individual state population.

appropriations—money set aside to spend on specific projects.

ballots—a voting system in which pieces of paper or other devices are used to record election choices.

batteries—warships' guns or other heavy artillery.

blockading—using ships or forces to prevent supplies from reaching an enemy.

Cabinet—people appointed by the president to head government departments and advise the president.

ceded—yielded possession.

circuit court—a traveling court that hears cases at different locations throughout the territory it covers.

compromiser—person who balances arguments or makes concessions in order to reach agreement.

dark horse—candidate whose nomination is a surprise.

draft law—a law that mandates compulsory military service for citizens.

electors—delegates from the states who choose the U.S. president and vice president.

electoral votes—each state's electors cast their votes for president and vice president of the United States. The larger a state's population, the more electoral votes it has.

emancipated—freed from bondage or restraint.

French Quarter—the historic central neighborhood of New Orleans.

garrison—a military post or the troops stationed there.

habeas corpus—an arrested person's right to be brought before a court to challenge the legality of the detention.

lobbied—tried to influence politicians or officials.

magnate—influential or powerful person, especially in a business or industry.

partisan—rigidly following a political party line.

plank—article or principle stated in a political platform.

platform—declaration of the principles and ideas of a political party or candidate.

president-elect—person who has been elected president but has not yet taken office.

promulgation—to make known by publically proclaiming.

proviso—condition, restriction, or stipulation, often in a legal document.

resolutions—formal expressions of opinion or intent by a body such as the U.S. Congress.

secede—withdraw from an organization or alliance.

siege—blockade designed to force a town or fortress to surrender.

sovereignty—power of a sovereign, such as a king; or popular self government.

surveyor—a person who measures distances, heights, and angles of land so that it can be mapped and divided into portions for sale.

tariffs—government-imposed charges on imported or exported goods.

union—the United States of America. During the Civil War, the Union was made up of those states that supported the U.S. Constitution and opposed the seceded states of the Confederacy.

BIBLIOGRAPHY

Baker, Jean H. *Mary Todd Lincoln: A Biography*. New York: W. W. Norton & Co., 1987.

Boorstin, Daniel J. *The Americans: The National Experience*. New York: Random House, 1965.

Carpenter, F. B. *The Inner Life of Abraham Lincoln: Six Months at the White House*. Lincoln, Nebraska: University of Nebraska Press, 1995.

Catton, Bruce. *The Civil War*. Boston: Houghton Mifflin Company, 1960.

Donald, David Herbert. *"We Are Lincoln Men": Abraham Lincoln and His Friends*. New York: Simon & Schuster, 2003.

Goodwin, Doris Kearns. *Team of Rivals: The Political Genius of Abraham Lincoln*. New York: Simon & Schuster, 2005

Keneally, Thomas. *Abraham Lincoln*. New York: Viking, 2003.

Langdon, William Chauncy. *Everyday Things in American Life, 1776–1876*. New York: Charles Scribner's Sons, 1951.

McPherson, James. *Battle Cry of Freedom: The Civil War Era*. New York: Oxford University Press, 1988.

Miller, William Lee. *Lincoln's Virtues: An Ethical Biography*. New York: Vintage Books, 2003.

Oates, Stephen B. *Abraham Lincoln: The Man Behind the Myths.* New York: Harper & Row, 1984.

Oates, Stephen B. *With Malice Toward None: The Life of Abraham Lincoln.* New York: Harper & Row, 1977.

Wilson, Douglas L. Honor's Voice: *The Transformation of Abraham Lincoln.* New York. Alfred A. Knopf, 1998.

Winkle, Kenneth J. The Young Eagle: *The Rise of Abraham Lincoln.* Dallas, Texas: Taylor Publishing Co., 2001.

About the Author

E. B. Phillips is the former European editor of Time Life Books. As a freelancer, she has written many books on such subjects as history, mythology and folklore, gardening, and cookery. She lives in Washington, D. C.

Image Credits

© CORBIS: 29, 51, 73, 75, 83

© Bettmann/CORBIS: 3, 17, 22, 46, 49, 72, 82 (top and bottom), 91

© Medford Historical Society Collection/CORBIS: 96

Photo by Kean Collection/Getty Images: 20

Photo by MPI/Getty Images: 31

Photo by Ralph Crane//Time Life Pictures/Getty Images: 25

The Granger Collection, New York: 5, 6 (top and bottom), 7, 10, 12, 18, 30, 33, 53, 56, 57, 62, 64, 69, 77, 78, 84, 90, 104, 106, 107, 111, 119

Photo by Sarah Gurfein: 118

From the collection of Keya Morgan of Keya Gallery in New York: 44 (bottom), 79

Library of Congress: 4, 19, 21, 36, 39, 42, 43, 45, 48, 55, 63, 66, 76, 81, 85, 88, 89, 92, 93, 95, 98, 100, 102, 103, 108, 112, 113, 114, 115, 116

Lincoln North: The Joseph N. Nathanson Collection of Lincolniana; Rare Books and Special Collections Division; McGill University Libraries, Montreal, Canada: 9

Northern Illinois University Libraries: 14

Courtesy of Picture History: 26, 28, 38, 44 (top), 50, 109

Cover art: © The Corcoran Gallery of Art/CORBIS

Index